HANDS
ALL AROUND

HANDS ALL AROUND

QUILTS FROM MANY NATIONS

Robert Bishop, Karey P. Bresenhan, and Bonnie Leman

E. P. DUTTON   NEW YORK

Hands All Around was selected as the title for this book because of its evocative imagery: joining the hands that hold the needles and rock the cradles into a circle of worldwide friendship. *Hands All Around*, a traditional term used in square dancing, is also the name of a nineteenth-century quilt pattern.

NOTE ABOUT DETAIL ILLUSTRATIONS

Page i: detail from figure 51, page 62
Pages 1, 2, 3, 7, 104: details from figure 50, page 61

Book design by Marilyn Rey

First published, 1987, in the United States by E. P. Dutton. / All rights reserved under International and Pan-American Copyright Conventions. / No part of this book may be reproduced or transmitted in any form or by any means, electronic or mechanical, including photocopy, recording, or any storage and retrieval system now known or to be invented, without permission in writing from the publishers, except by a reviewer who wishes to quote brief passages in connection with a review written for inclusion in a magazine, newspaper, or broadcast. / Published simultaneously in Canada by Fitzhenry & Whiteside Limited, Toronto. / W / Published in the United States by E. P. Dutton, a division of New American Library, 2 Park Avenue, New York, N.Y. 10016. / Printed in Spain. / Library of Congress Catalog Card Number: 86-71896 / ISBN: 0-525-24504-9 (cloth); ISBN: 0-525-48280-6 (DP).
10 9 8 7 6 5 4 3 2 1 First Edition

CONTENTS

PREFACE

Hands All Around: Quilts from Many Nations is a celebration of the remarkable craftsmanship and design skills of needlework artists from the many countries that have enjoyed a long quilting tradition or that have recently developed one. It is the first major visual documentation of worldwide quiltmaking as it is practiced by the most skilled of today's quilt artists.

This book was inspired by the exhibition, "Hands All Around: International Quilts," mounted at the International Quilt Festival in Houston, Texas, in October 1985. The exhibit, which featured fifty quilts by forty-two quiltmakers from seventeen countries, was curated by Karey Bresenhan and Bonnie Leman, and the presentation was sponsored by *Quilter's Newsletter Magazine.* Karey Bresenhan noted, "Quilts have become their own international language. They communicate love of beauty and pride in workmanship just as clearly as if they could speak aloud.... The techniques are the same the world over, but the images vary from country to country. Quilters surrounded by the majesty of the Swiss Alps or the dignity of an ocean surrounding an island country cannot help but be influenced in their designs. Quilters living in a land famed for its diamond mines or its African tribes cannot help but be inspired by that heritage. The resulting mix is rich and complex.

It adds significantly to our vision of quilting as an art form that can unite the world in appreciation for beauty just as the Olympics unite the world in appreciation for athletics."

While we admire the ability of the quiltmaker to design with undeniable clarity and stitch with sure hands these thoroughly satisfying works of art, it is important to remember that nearly all of the textiles illustrated are viewed by their makers as showpieces and they are seldom intended for use on family beds. In fact, the pragmatic reasons for making a quilt that were so compelling in the seventeenth, eighteenth, and nineteenth centuries have all but disappeared in many countries. Today, most people purchase a blanket or a comforter to use as a bedcover, but hang their quilts, stretched and framed like valuable paintings, on their walls. These art quilts are nearly always made from new fabrics purchased for the specific purpose of making a quilt.

Function, however, is still a concern for some contemporary quilters. As in the past, quilts for daily use are sometimes pieced from scraps of cloth salvaged from worn-out clothing and other fabrics saved especially for the purpose.

The traditional quilting bee is still very much alive in

small towns and cities throughout the world. A recent press report on a YWCA quilting bee held in New York City related that 300 individuals actually did quilting while twice that number wandered about the room, observing the work. The Western Australian Quilters' Association reports that "the majority of our 340-strong membership spent many enjoyable hours around the quilt frame" to provide quilts for some of the State's pioneer dwellings.

In the United States, England, Australia, France, Japan, West Germany, Ireland, and other countries over 1,000 quilt guilds, some with several hundred members, continue the quilting-bee traditions in well-organized, regularly scheduled meetings where members work together, learn from one another, and enjoy the social aspects of intensely interested participants.

Traditionally, the appliqué quilt has been considered the most difficult and beautiful form of quilt artistry. There are some quiltmakers and collectors who feel that the appliqué quilt lacks the inspiration of the pieced quilt and perhaps shows less inventive design, although "for show" or "best" quilts have nearly always been appliquéd. Few nineteenth-century American appliqués matched the splendid, if somewhat standardized examples stitched by the ladies of Baltimore, Maryland, and surrounding areas in the 1830–1860 period.

Piecework continues to produce stunning, even astonishing, geometric designs so popular with collectors today. As is seen in the majority of the quilts illustrated in this book, the technique makes it possible to achieve a seemingly endless variety of patterns. Enthusiasm for vivid, bold abstractions in a contemporary palette has created many new visual solutions. It is fascinating that the craft of quilting, which has survived for centuries in many countries, enjoyed a strong revival in nineteenth-century America but didn't reach its fullest expression until after the middle of the twentieth century. Its most recent revival, begun in the 1960s, has caused needle-women around the world once again to take their needles and create quilted art.

Nationalism and personal experiences play an increasingly important role in the development of quilt design today. No longer are standardized patterns, easily copied and passed along to friends, as important as they once were. The illustrations in *Hands All Around* indicate that many of the best contemporary quilters rightly consider themselves, and are viewed as, needlework artists united by a universal desire to craft beautiful textiles. With *Hands All Around* we celebrate their remarkable talents, their skills, and their success that is an inspiration to us all.

ROBERT BISHOP

INTRODUCTION

Lost in the memory of time, the origins and heritage of patchwork, appliqué, and quilting around the world provide a fascinating mystery full of the romance of long-lost cultures and far-flung places.

To unravel that mystery requires tracing back into early civilization, seeking out the influences of culture and tradition, and discovering the strong commonality of design that links nation to nation, people to people, and generation to generation.

That instinctive commonality of design is still evident, as quiltmakers around the world create contemporary abstract quilts, one-of-a-kind designs that in no way resemble traditional quilts yet still reflect subconscious ties to the design heritage of early needle artists.

Even though she may have no prior knowledge of quilting or patchwork, even though she may not have seen a quilting book until long after she had started work with cloth, even though she may work in almost complete isolation from the influences of both the past and the present, today's quiltmaker creates her quilts with variations on the same methods known to the early stitchers. Indeed, her designs show instinctive kinship to the historic geometrics and natural forms seen in fiber designs long before the birth of Christ.

Only fragments of the world's early patchwork re-main, along with images captured in ancient paintings and carvings. These serve as clues, but they do not solve the puzzle. However, they reaffirm the timeless quality of patchwork and quilting, the certainty that men and women from earliest days have sought to combine the need for thrift with the urge to create and to decorate. All over the world, different folk groups found the same solution to that need. Today many contemporary quiltmakers cite these same reasons for turning to patchwork and quilting. Each of these groups, working within different limitations of skill or materials, has shown how the resultant technique and form are closely linked with inherited tradition and the prevailing sense of beauty.

The Nbebele tribeswoman in Africa who paints her hut freehand with inherited geometric designs that mirror quilt borders; the Swiss farmers of years past who decorated their barn doors in the Bern canton with the same concentric diamonds that later found fame in their descendants' Amish quilts; the nomads who packed up their patchwork tents to roam the desert: from all of these sources, rich and varied as the cultures that created them, stem the origins of patchwork and quilting in the world today. Common designs that seem to spring from the collective unconscious tie together the work of people long passed from the earth with the work of people scattered around the world as we know it today. Diamonds, squares, triangles, hexagons, octagons, circles—all are utilized with startling similarity and repetitive effectiveness in the work of isolated tribesmen and sophisticated city dwellers.

Although quilting, patchwork, and appliqué were sometimes inextricably linked in many cultures, they are not always synonymous. A quilt does not have to be made of patchwork or contain appliqué, just as patchwork or appliqué work does not have to be quilted. Making that distinction is important to understanding the history and influence of these needle arts.

One fact, however, seems certain: contrary to popular myth, none of these three important needle arts originated in Colonial America. Instead, all three methods were highly developed long before the existence of written history and may be traced back as far as the times of the pharaohs in ancient Egypt, one of the earliest centers of civilization. The earliest example of quilting is found in a carved ivory figurine dating around 3400 B.C. and discovered at the Temple of Osiris in 1903. It depicts an Egyptian pharaoh cloaked in a mantle carved in deep relief with diamond patterns typical of quilting designs. The depth of the carving suggests the thick padding needed to create insulation, the primary reason for the development of quilting. The figurine is now found in the British Museum in London.

The earliest reference to patchwork is also an image— a wall painting of an Egyptian sailing vessel with sails made of squares of colored fabrics joined in a checkerboard pattern with a chevron border. This painting, found at Thebes, has been dated between 1198 and 1167 B.C., at the time of Rameses III.

An actual example of early appliqué, rather than an image, still exists and may be found in the collection of the Boulak Museum in Cairo. Dated about 980 B.C., this is the ceremonial canopy of an Egyptian queen's funeral tent. It is constructed of gazelle hides dyed in the soft, rich colors typical of vegetable dyes. Cutout shapes of flowers and early symbols are applied to the surface of the tent, obviously as a form of decoration. Some of these same designs may still be found in twentieth-century Egyptian appliqué.

This canopy is almost 1,000 years older than the next-oldest existing example of appliqué, a small quilted carpet or floor covering discovered by the Koslov expedition to Mongolia in 1924 and believed to have been made between 100 B.C. and A.D. 200. It was found on the floor of a tomb just as it might have been used on the floor of a nomad chieftain's tent. The piece is skillfully quilted in a repetitive pattern of large clockwise and counterclockwise spirals, with a narrow border of interlocking geometrics surrounding the center. Appliquéd shapes of trees and animals are found along the border, which is quilted with diagonal and crosshatch lines. It is now housed in the Leningrad Department of the Institute of Archaeology, part of the Russian Academy of Sciences.

Nomadic tribes carried quilting, appliqué, and patchwork throughout the Eastern cultures, and between the first century B.C. and the second century A.D., *pa ndau*, with its sophisticated tuck-and-fold appliqué, and reverse appliqué, was developing among the isolated Hmong peoples of Southeast Asia. The ancient Persians, many of whom were also nomads, had wide influence on quiltmaking, specifically on the development of the Tree of Life design which is based on traditional Persian carpets. The Persians also developed a method of inlaid appliqué that closely resembles mosaic tile and looks very much like work being done today.

The earliest surviving example of patchwork, dating between the sixth and ninth centuries, was found early in the twentieth century by the Stein expedition as it was conducting an archaeological survey for the Indian government. The expedition explored the Serindia region, a remote area beyond the Ganges River, where they found examples of early patchwork in a walled-up chapel. The chapel was part of the Caves of the 1,000 Buddhas located on an old trade route that stretched from the silk-growing areas of China into Central Asia and even farther into the West. Among the treasures found by the archaeologists was a large votive hanging pieced of rectangles of multicolored and figured silks, damasks, and embroidery. These pieces were probably offerings left by travelers. Also found in the cave was a small pieced silk bag made of three rows of squares and triangles constructed by a method identical to what is known today as English piecing. It looks almost exactly like silk patchwork made around 1890, at the height of the Victorian period. It requires only a small stretch of the imagination to perceive the undeniable link between Eastern and Western patchwork and quilting.

During the Middle Ages, patchwork, appliqué, and quilting were brought back to Western civilization by the Crusaders returning from their holy wars against the infidel in the East. Patchwork was primarily used to create richly decorated banners and heraldic devices, and quilting was favored for the construction of defensive body armor worn over or under metal armor, so that the heavily quilted material absorbed the impact of weapons such as arrows. After the development of guns, quilted armor was discarded because it provided no protection against modern weaponry. Decorative quilted clothing continued to be in favor, however, and in recent times, a replica of a quilted "jack" (an early jacket), worn by the Black Prince, has hung over his tomb in Canterbury Cathedral. It is made of red and blue velvet embroidered with the Royal Arms of England and entirely quilted with vertical lines.

Whole-cloth quilting was also probably used for bedcovers at this time, but because of the utilitarian nature of such pieces, none has survived except in literary references: "The quilt was of a check-board pattern of two sorts of silk cloth," quoted from a book of French poems, *La Lai del Desire*, written in the twelfth or thirteenth century. However, the earliest existing example of a bed quilt is a Sicilian piece made near the end of the fourteenth century. It is made of quilted linen padded with wool and features scenes from the legend of Tristan, quilted and stuffed in high relief. Three such pieces exist—one in the Victoria and Albert Museum, another in the Bargello Museum in Florence, and the third in a private collection in Florence—and opinion is divided about whether or not these are three separate quilts or three pieces from one quilt.

Written records from this period indicate that quilting was also frequently used for such household furnishings as bed hangings. However, from that time on, bed quilts grew increasingly popular among aristocrats and peasants. They were also being produced in several parts of the world, including India. Sea-going Portuguese merchants sent word from India in the early sixteenth century that white and colored quilts (produced by painting designs), as well as bed hangings, were being made there. India had a great influence on the development of quiltmaking in the world because of its rich profusion of colors, intricate designs, and extensive use of borders. Even Indian book illustrations and architecture provided a rich source for quilt designs, and their production of the first chintz fabric had a long-lasting effect on floral appliqué and Broderie Perse.

In European countries, most bed quilts were of the whole-cloth type in a single color, and were elaborately designed, sometimes with corded or stuffed work. During this general period, a sixteenth-century German quilt was made of heavy linen with exotic animals on a stippled background, a Spanish quilt was listed in the inventory of Louis XIV of France, and Swedish work contained examples of elaborate quilting patterns combined with embroidery stitches, all executed in white on white.

Patchwork and quilting continued to develop in the Eastern cultures during this period also. For example, what is known as the "Turkish booty" found today in the Badisches Landesmuseum in Karlsruhe, Germany,

contains fragments of a Turkish ceremonial tent from the Ottoman Empire of the seventeenth century. Its background contains multicolored silks and satins pieced together. Over this are appliquéd floral motifs made of mutlicolored silk taffeta and gilded leather. This elaborate piece reflects the direct effect of a change in interior architecture around that time. Powerful color combinations achieved favor, and glazed tiles with heavy encrustations of marble and plaster were often used as architectural embellishments. This was in direct contrast to the sparsely furnished interiors of the past, which often utilized rugs as their sole decoration. This trend toward elaboration had a direct effect on the design of textiles from that period forward.

This elaborate effect was magnified in English quilts of the eighteenth century, with the development of the complex medallion-style quilt, which used piecing only in borders around an appliqué center. Clamshell designs also originated at this time.

Japanese patchwork in the seventeenth and eighteenth centuries consisted primarily of costume design. Kosodes (kosode is the old name for kimono) and Noh costumes were fashioned by piecing together different blocks of fabrics, the earliest form of Japanese patchwork. Sometimes the patchwork effect was so desirable that fabrics were printed or dyed to achieve the look without the effort of piecing. Certain types of kimonos were pieced together from two different kimonos, with each half of the costume having an entirely different design. This also allowed the economical use of damaged kimonos, which could be cut apart and reassembled with a different half, emphasizing the patchwork effect while making thrifty use of the expensive fabrics usually found in kimonos. Since the entire concept of the kimono was so strictly controlled by custom and tradition at that time, the patchwork effect provided a pleasing change of pace and yet was socially acceptable. This effect was probably not the result of "making do," because these kimonos were usually owned only by the well-to-do, but instead was created specifically for its aesthetic excitement, so different from the serenity usually expressed in Japanese art forms.

For example, a kimono might combine imported materials—silver and gold, brocade and damask—and the value of the finished garment would be found not only in the expensive materials but more important, in the balance of color and form—a distinctly contemporary trend quiltmakers today understand quite well.

The peasant classes in early Japan were forbidden by law to buy expensive silks, nor could they afford to, so for economical reasons they patched old fabrics and quilted them to make their garments last longer. Even today, a Japanese custom calls for a patchwork kimono jacket or vest to be made on the occasion of special birthdays (such as the sixtieth, seventieth, and eightieth), with the garment having the same number of patches as the person's age.

Quilted clothing, especially petticoats and waistcoats, enjoyed a revival in the eighteenth and nineteenth centuries in many parts of the world, especially England and Europe. In Syria, garments resembling long coats were embellished with reversible patterns of cord quilting. In south Wales, it was considered a mark of respectability to be buried in a quilted black petticoat, and by the late nineteenth century, owning a large number of quilted petticoats was a status symbol, particularly in country towns. Quilting parties were sometimes held in Northern Ireland at this time, and in Wales, "strippie" quilts, made of alternating strips of two colors, were developed. During the nineteenth century in south Wales, professional quilters traveled through the countryside planning quilting patterns and making quilts for the families that provided them with lodging. Emphasis was always on the counterpane side with its fancy quilting design, but the women sometimes had to settle for patchwork backs, hence "strippie" quilts.

In certain areas of Scotland, it was the custom to burn the bedstead and all the bedding, including the quilts and blankets, when someone died in the bed; this practice was carried over into Canada with the arrival of the Scottish immigrants. Home weaving was also prevalent in Scotland, and homespun quilts are frequently found there and in areas settled by Scots.

Quilting came to America in the seventeenth century, when the first Colonists arrived. It took root in fertile ground, and has since flourished to such an extent that the United States has been the leader in quilting innovations for more than a hundred years. The first American quilts were undoubtedly made of simple patchwork because the hardship in which the Colonists lived and worked would have left no time for fancy stitching. Warmth was the overriding concern in New England's bitter cold. Fabric itself was scarce and every piece had to be used until it fell apart. No American quilt from this difficult period exists today, but beautiful pieced and appliqué quilts survive from the first quarter of the eighteenth century, proving that needlework was a highly valued skill in early America.

Significant evidence indicates that block-style patchwork and appliqué originated in nineteenth-century America and were later carried back to England and Europe. By the mid-1850s, thousands of patchwork and appliqué patterns had been designed specifically for making the block-style quilts that covered the nation's beds.

Quilting in America is still widely practiced, nurtured by a rich heritage of workmanship, ingenuity, legend, and tradition that has been chronicled extensively in the many books written on the development of quilting in this country. Today, the United States leads the world in quilting businesses, magazines, conferences, shows, contests, supplies, books, collectors, and quilters. Quilting is an art the American people have taken to their hearts from the beginning.

Tracing the symbiosis of patchwork, appliqué, and quilting throughout the world is fascinating and as full of complexities as quilters are full of contradictions. Folk groups all over the world have expanded the possibilities implicit in the combination of thrift and decoration by developing their own quilt traditions. In each case, behind the actual techniques and forms used can be found the inherited traditions and the natural evolution of a collective aesthetic.

Today, quilters in many lands approach quilting with different purposes and widely varying backgrounds. They work under unusual conditions, and their motivations vary as dramatically as their quilts.

They ply their art in open-air houses on Polynesian islands, or they are closeted in the bleak Arctic winters when the sun rarely shines. They work as strangers in strange lands, uprooted and moved to far-flung places by jobs or family, or they work in ancestral homes surrounded by centuries of family heritage. One wealthy European quilter has added an entire story to her flat-roofed house, which provides her with a huge, light-filled atelier, where even the floor is white. Here she has superb working conditions in "a room of her own." Other quilters, without that luxury, work in cramped, two-room apartments where spreading out fabrics to design a quilt creates chaos and sometimes the floor is the only available work space. One quilter in West Germany, a transplanted American, shares an atelier with her husband—he paints while she patches.

According to Mary Penders, an American quilting teacher who has taught in many other lands, "The solitude and independence of many women who are working in isolation from other quilters is significant. These women appear to be highly motivated to pursue clearly defined goals without benefit of the social and commercial quilt world. Lack of communication with other quilters, prohibitive distances from supply centers, and straitened financial circumstances have not been a hindrance to their production of noteworthy quilts."

At times, their quilting is a solace, a comfort, as in the case of the quilter who pieces and quilts by the bedside of her semi-invalid husband. While she quilts, he reads to her, hours at a time. In the words of one West German quilter: "Many quilts bridge times of sorrow and bring color to lives not wholly joyous. And when the bad times are over, one has a thing of beauty in their stead."

At other times, quiltmaking could almost be said to be a matter of national pride, as Mary Penders points out when she explains that "established quilt artists are in the forefront of the movement to develop a national quilt identity that is particular to their cultural heritage. Many quilters in other countries are strongly influenced by physical geography and, often, by the design heritage of the original inhabitants of their lands. European quilters are motivated to establish a personal identity in their quilt art, as is seen in the expressionist content of many of the German quilts, wherein ideas and emotions are symbolically rendered. The originality of many German and Swiss quilts is all the more striking to American eyes accustomed to viewing such quilts in proximity to traditional forms rather than in place of them."

The quiltmakers have their own private reasons for turning to quilting: the French quilter who is compelled to create something as a unique personal statement; the Dutch quilter who seeks to capture the perfection of the past; the Japanese quilter who combines her country's traditional embroidery with brilliant contemporary quilt images; the New Zealand quilter whose location forces her to work in virtual isolation from widespread influences in quilt design; the East German quilter who, finding it impossible to obtain appropriate fabrics, develops her patchwork using hand-dyed raw silk. All of these quiltmakers respond in individual, idiosyncratic ways to the need to create. They turn to fabrics, needle, and thread as naturally as artists in the past turned to brush, paints, and canvas. Yet their work is more than the sum of their own experiences, their own individualistic creations; indeed, their work is a direct link to the stitchers of ancient history, to the traditions of their people, and to the sense of beauty accepted in their culture.

KAREY P. BRESENHAN

Note to the reader: Inasmuch as the purpose of this book is to present quilts as works of art, the dimensions given for each quilt, where known, follow the style used for paintings, where the vertical dimension always precedes the horizontal.

GALLERY
OF
INTERNATIONAL QUILTS

1. *Autumn Winds* by Margaret E. Hannaford, Golden Beach, Queensland, Australia. 1985. 76″ x 90″. Cotton, cotton-blend fabrics. Hand-pieced and hand-quilted. Inspired by an autumn visit to Canberra, the national capital of Australia, the quiltmaker tried to capture the movement of the falling leaves caught by dry swirling winds sweeping across the garden city. "While making this quilt, my mood went from pure joy to utter frustration and back again as I tried to maintain constant form in my design," the quiltmaker explains. In this original free-form design, she shows her dedication to her adopted craft, originally a substitute for her first love, pottery, which she had to abandon because of illness. Now, as she says, "There are long periods of time when I do little else but quilt. I am fortunate to have a very understanding husband who happily relieves me of many household chores when he can see I am so involved in a quilt that I can hardly bear to put it down." In the past three years, she has taught more than seventy women in her area to quilt, where her home overlooks both Pumicestone Passage and Caloundra Headland to the Pacific Ocean, and she helped to establish the Caloundra Quilters and served as its first president.

2. *Cactus Dunes* by Joan McKenzie, Karalee, Queensland, Australia. 1985. 170 x 210 cm (64⅜″ x 79½″). Machine-pieced, hand-appliquéd, hand-quilted. Combining traditional blocks with contemporary patchwork is a favorite technique for this quiltmaker, who also prefers to work in series. This quilt is part of her current series featuring desert tones and earth colors. She has captured the stark beauty of the Australian outback, the miles of dunes that know no water, in the elegance of this piece and has conveyed the ever-present wind that sculpts the dunes in her choice of quilting designs. This series is an abrupt departure from the quiltmaker's earlier fascination with the sea that surrounds her island nation. "I discovered patchwork while working as a crafts teacher six years ago," she states, and explains that she is primarily self-taught. She adds that "most of the old quilts in Australia came on the ships from England."

3. *Shaded Peaks* by Barbara Meredith, Armidale, New South Wales, Australia. 1985. 118″ x 90″. Cotton and poly-cotton fabrics. Machine-pieced, hand-quilted. The quiltmaker spent eight months in Perth in Western Australia, where she was impressed by the "rugged beauty of the mountain peaks, the tradition of diamond mining, and the fabulous colors in the morning and evening lights." She created this quilt with its 630 equilateral triangles, around fifty shades of blue and rose pieced into diamond-shaped blocks, and mountain peak quilting to reflect the excitement and color of the area in which diamonds are still mined. She was initially inspired to take up quilting after seeing Hawaiian quilters at work on a visit to the islands. She later enrolled in quilting conferences and seminars in the United States and Canada and has only recently attended workshops in Australia and New Zealand. The quilters in her region are planning a 1988 symposium to celebrate Australia's Bicentennial and hope to tour the quilt exhibits through the country regions of the nation.

4. *Australian Birds* by Margaret Rolfe, Curtin, A.C.T., Australia. 1981. 112 x 112 cm (42⁷/₁₆″ x 42⁷/₁₆″). Cotton, poly-cotton fabrics; polyester batting. Hand-appliquéd and hand-quilted. Nine of Australia's most famous birds are depicted on this quilt, which uses narrow strips of brown sashing to give the appearance of a window through which the birds may be seen. "This quilt is special to me," says the quiltmaker, "because almost all of the birds can be seen in my own garden from time to time . . . like the galahs who perch on the power line just outside my kitchen window. Of all my quilts, this is my favourite. I made it very quickly, in an intense two-month period." The quiltmaker, author of *Australian Patchwork*, has received two grants from the Crafts Board of the Australia Council to study and research the history of patchwork in that country and has spent five years in documenting and photographing Australian patchwork dating from 1788 to the present. Her studies have revealed that while there is no real tradition of quilting in Australia, there is certainly a rich heritage of patchwork, Crazy quilts, and Log Cabin construction.

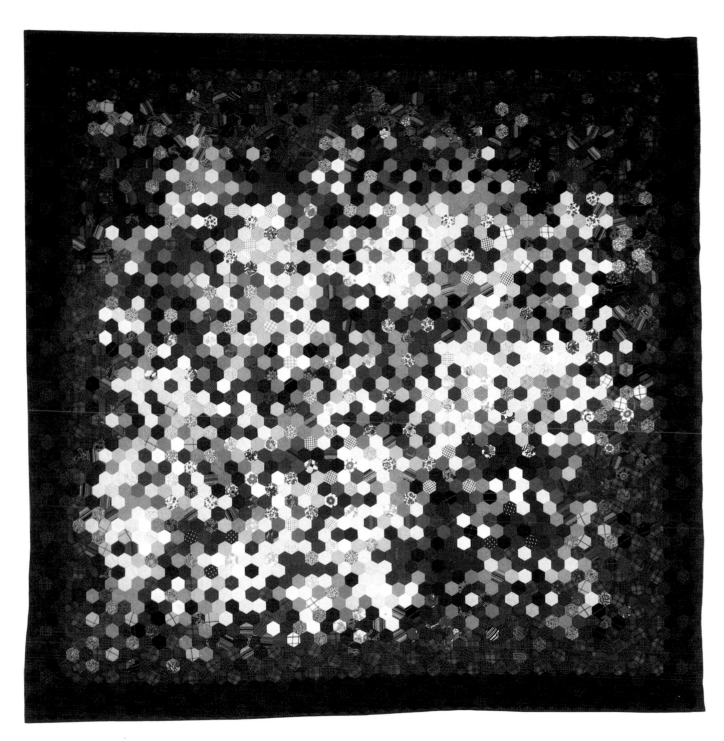

5. *My Three Sons* by Nancy Tingey, New Town, Tasmania, Australia. 1980. 90″ x 90″. Cotton, poly-cotton, wool fabrics. Hand-pieced and tied. The triads of 1″ hexagons are used by the quiltmaker to represent both her own life with her three sons and that of her mother-in-law who was also the mother of three sons. The overall quilt design produces the effect of random distribution, even though the triads have actually been carefully arranged. This contrast "symbolizes the structured and yet spontaneous patterns of events which make up our lives," explains the quiltmaker. Entirely pieced by hand using the English paper-piecing method, the quilt is a type of friendship quilt containing nothing but fabric that was given to the quilter by family and friends in England and Australia. It was started during a trip to the Australian outback and later finished as a gift to her husband's mother on his fortieth birthday. The quiltmaker's work reflects the influences of England, where she lived for thirty years, as well as Australia. "I was always attracted to any kind of patchwork—crazy paving, stone walls, jigsaws," she recalls. Trained in fine art, she "found patchwork to be the answer to making large art-works while traveling with and caring for a young family."

6. *Red Centre* by Ruth C. Walter, Hamilton, Victoria, Australia. 1982. 230 x 172 cm (87⅛″ x 65⅛″). Poly-cotton fabrics, heavy batting. Hand-appliquéd, hand-quilted. Depicting the sand dunes, desert, and rock formations of the center of Australia, this quilt was made as a gift for the quilter's sixteen-year-old son after a family trip to central Australia. "We camped at Ayers Rock and explored much of the countryside," reports the quilter, who cited the trip as the source for her design for this piece. She specifically selected a very heavy batting to give the desired three-dimensional effect emphasized by the free-form quilting, and the vibrant red and brown re-create the contour lines, the red dirt typical of an iron-producing region, and geographic shapes of the area. The quilt-maker learned to quilt during a two-year stay in Philadelphia, Pennsylvania, in 1975–1977.

7. *Barrier Reef* by Jane Wilson, Brisbane, Queensland, Australia. 1984. 61½″ x 62″. Cotton and poly-cotton fabrics. Machine-pieced, hand-embroidered, hand-quilted. As a child, the quiltmaker was fascinated by the Great Barrier Reef and the many colors of blue seen in the sea. She has translated that youthful memory into a bold, vivid picture of life beneath the sea with its striations of blues and greens and the dimensional images of the fish superimposed over the water. The design is centered on a large eight-point starfish block embellished with embroidery, and the twelve angular fish are crazy-patched. "This quilt is the result of an uninterrupted two-week Summer School held in Toowoomba, Queensland. The workshop encouraged me to design and execute a quilt on an Australian theme. The fabric colours used in the background reminded me strongly of the water surrounding the Great Barrier Reef; also, I am fascinated by quilts where the background changes. Many different coloured quilting threads were used to link up the levels of water."

8. *Flowers and Leaves* by Helen Gritscher, Thaur, Tirol, Austria. 1984. 165 x 135 cm (62½" x 51⅛"). Cotton and poly-cotton fabrics, polyester batting. Machine-pieced, hand-quilted. Intricate, curved-seam piecing and subtle colors add elegance to this abstract quilt, made by an Australian-turned-Austrian. An original design, the pattern has a contemporary flair overlaid with the complexity of an ancient political culture. The flower design was created from a quarter-circle. "I really have to be considered as Austrian since I started quilting here, although I knew about it in Australia," explains the quilter. "What is quilting in Austria? A few know about it, but hardly anyone does it! I know of only two women in Tirol," she adds. "Isolation is splendid sometimes, but it can also be frustrating. Still, quilting is always a creative relaxation for me." The quilt was made for her son, then seven, who selected the colors himself.

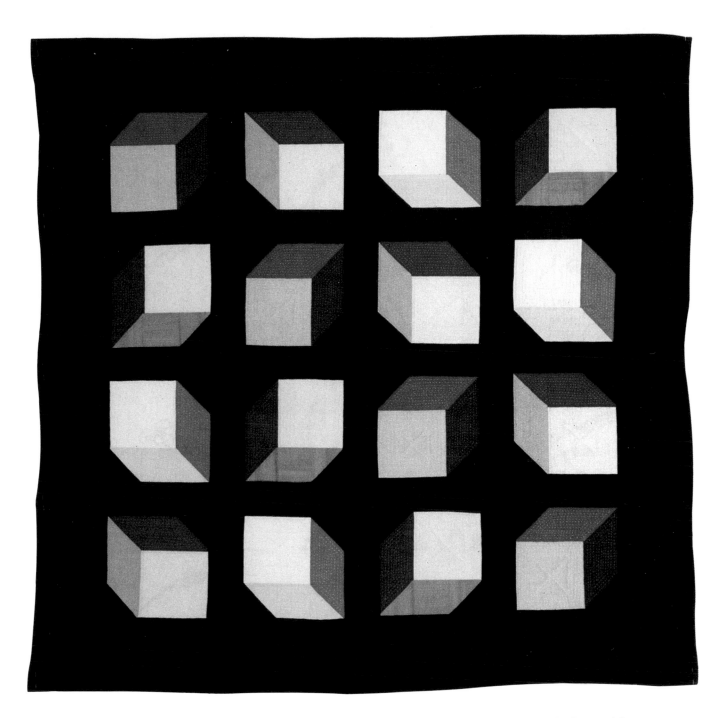

9. *Flying Boxes* by Josephine Vercauteren, Antwerp, Belgium. 120 x 120 cm (45½″ x 45½″). Cotton fabrics. Machine-pieced and hand-quilted. Through the manipulation of color and shape, the quiltmaker has created a fascinating study of motion and dimension. The quilt is closely related to the traditional Baby's Block pattern, but reflects an idiosyncratic approach to the basic block design. The light-filled colors are framed and emphasized by the black background. Completely self-taught in both art and quilting, the quiltmaker is "an autodidact" who works out her own variations of traditional patterns by sketching hundreds to study the inter-action between colors, blocks, and patterns, then cutting out part of the sketch to try at different angles and in different combinations. "Sometimes a whole new pattern emerges by accentuating some line or parts," she says. Her work reflects the natural integration of cultural influences that exist in Flanders, in the northern part of Belgium, a country situated between Holland, Germany, and France. The quiltmaker's interest in creating art stems from her surroundings in Antwerp with its many beautiful old Gothic and Baroque churches and museums. "I was educated by my father to love all those old churches—he showed me all the great expressions of Flemish art and craftsmanship. I am very sure that the basis of my love for beauty was laid in my youth, and perhaps my quilts are the expression of that love."

10. *Little Town in Minas Gerais* by Barbara Schaeffter, São Paulo, Brazil. 1985. 44″ x 45″. Cotton fabrics. Hand-pieced, machine-pieced, hand-quilted. Clouds hover over a timeless town cooled by mountain breezes quilted into the pieced sky in this original design. Minas Gerais is an upland state, about the size of Texas, located between Rio and Brasilia, where gold and precious stones once lured miners to test their fortunes. Today, iron mines and industry have replaced the gold miners of the past, but small towns like this one still slumber on, evoking life in another century. One of New York quilting teacher Maria Belden's many international students, the quiltmaker has most effectively conveyed the architectural details of this colonial town: tiled roofs, quilted fountains, arched entryways framed with quilted vines, and the village church with its bell tower topped with a quilted cross.

11. *Amish Dancers* by Ann Bird, Toronto, Ontario, Canada. 1985. 60″ x 60″. Cotton fabrics, polyester batting. Strip-pieced, machine reverse appliquéd, hand-quilted. "I have long admired the colour relationships and simplicity of Amish quilts," states the quiltmaker in explaining her design. "This modern tribute combines the two images of dancers and stars which I have often used in previous quilts. I like to design my quilts from the centre and am fascinated with the myriad possibilities for pattern a star provides by repetition of any number of points." This quilt also continues her emphasis on the reverse side of her designs. "I add elements of design to the backs of my quilts to make them as visually appealing as the tops. The back of this quilt [see following illustration] is an abstract form expressing space and motion." Introduced to quiltmaking by observing a group of women quilting at a state fair, the quilter taught herself from books. She cites the shared U.S.-Canadian history of pioneer settlement as one of the major influences on the development of quilting in Canada, augmented by "the strong American influence of the past ten to fifteen years in movements such as the women's, ecological, craft, etc." The quiltmaker is a recognized Canadian fabric artist who has been awarded a government grant to pursue her art. She has exhibited her work internationally and frequently conducts seminars at U.S. and Canadian quilt symposia.

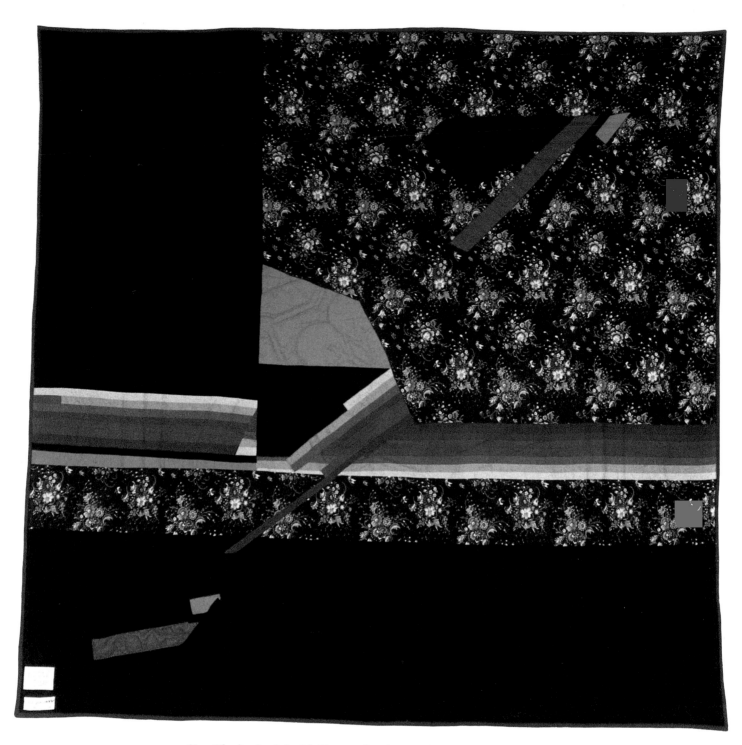

11a. The back of *Amish Dancers* by Ann Bird, illustrated in figure 11.

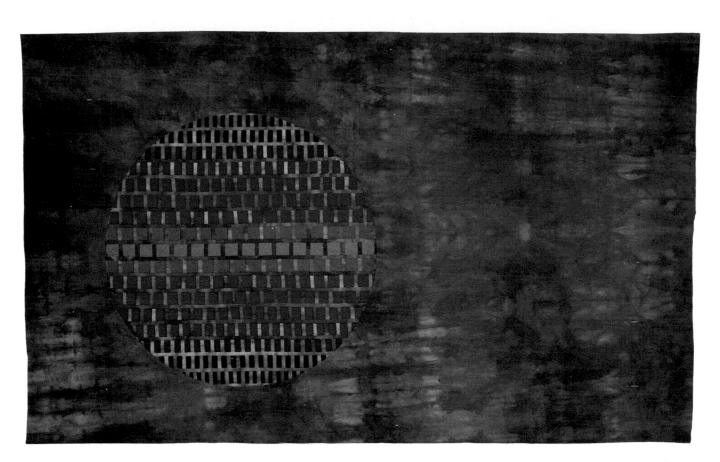

12. *Winter Planet* by Ann Bird, Ottawa, Ontario, Canada. 1985. 43″ x 71″. Strip-pieced and hand-quilted. The chill serenity of the world in winter is reflected in this original contemporary piece. The quiltmaker likes to use another geometric design on the reverse side of her works, as she has done with this piece (see also figs. 11 and 11a).

13. *Don's Quilt* by Winifrede Burry, Toronto, Ontario, Canada. 1980. 90″ x 72″. Cotton and poly-cotton fabrics. Hand-appliquéd, reverse appliquéd, hand-quilted. Native animals are depicted here in representations of designs created by Canadian native artists of the Woodland School: Norval Morriseau, Carl Ray, Isaac Bignell, and Inuit artist Kenojuak Ashevak. The quilt was made as a high school graduation gift for the quiltmaker's second son, Donald. According to her, "It is thanks to his constant encouragement that I am now completely 'hooked' on the wonderful work of our native and Inuit artists." After another of the quiltmaker's designs based on Inuit work won a first prize, she wrote the artist and received this reply—written in Inuit, which resembles nothing so much as hieroglyphics to the untrained eye: "I am so please that you won with my design. That's all I have to say, and good-bye. Even though I have never seen you before, I am happy."

14. *Communication* by Winifrede Burry, Toronto, Ontario, Canada. 1981. 88″ x 68″. Cotton and poly-cotton fabrics. Hand-appliquéd, reverse appliquéd, machine-pieced, hand-quilted. Based on a print, *Communication*, by Jackson Beardy, this quilt was made as a high school graduation gift for the quiltmaker's youngest son, John, who is very interested in the world of communication, both as a ham-radio operator and as a trained writer.

15. *The Peace Quilt* by Valerie Hearder, Mahone Bay, Nova Scotia, Canada. 1974–1979. Hand-pieced, hand-appliquéd, hand-quilted. Started in her native South Africa and finished five years later in Canada, this exciting piece reflects both the pulsating vitality of the quiltmaker's politically divided homeland and the chill serenity of life in the Arctic territories of her adopted country. The center is a small Buddhist peace flag, and the quilting designs are adapted from the Zulu symbol for "great peace." The quiltmaker has a lifelong affinity for the thousands of indigo prints found in Africa. When she left to marry and move to the Canadian Northwest Territories, only 200 miles from the Arctic Circle, with her went her African indigos. During that first terrible winter, she turned to her fabrics for comfort. "Those precious fabrics were my sanity through that winter that lasted eight months," she recalls. "They were the only familiar elements in a frozen world, a link to my native home." The quiltmaker's designs recall her heritage as a fifth-generation South African and her hopes for that country's future. "My mother still lives in South Africa, and she still sends me my beloved indigo-printed fabric, my only tangible link with my home country, for I am now a Canadian citizen. I know I can never go back, and I suppose my mother will leave in time. I feel sad for my country, but I've grown to love Canada, especially Nova Scotia. This is home now."

16. *Pink and Blue* by Sue Lent, Fruitvale, British Columbia, Canada. 1984. 235 x 180 cm (89″ x 68³/₁₆″). Hand-pieced. Constructed by the *English paper method*—which is "excessively boring," states the quiltmaker—each of the 4,525 pieces of fabric in this quilt top was laboriously basted around an exact 1¼″ paper template to obtain precise edges, then each hexagon was whipstitched to the next by hand. This method requires a separate template for every hexagon, and when antique examples of this "honeycomb" type of quilt are found, it is often possible to date the item by finding a year mentioned in the old newspapers or letters used to create the templates. *Pink and Blue* is a classic example of an international quilt: the English quiltmaker was living in France when she submitted the quilt for the book, and has since moved to British Columbia. Her artistry is evident in this quilt with its carefully designed color gradations, a difficult effect to achieve by the English piecing method. She has made several quilts by the same method, including one with 9,409 1″ squares. This is one of a pair of single-bed quilts; the mate, *Blue and Pink*, presents a different image because of the placement of the colors. The quiltmaker learned to quilt from her mother in England and started making patchwork at the age of twelve. She developed her unusual approach to hexagonal patchwork after obtaining a degree in fine arts.

17. *the third i storm centre* by Robin Morey, Harrow, Ontario, Canada. 1985. 100″ x104″. Cotton, poly-cotton, satin fabrics; polyester fleece batting. Strip-pieced. "Against a varied background of midnight blues, an imposing circular shape appears to leap from the flat surface as a whirling vortex culminating in what appears to be a huge single eye as it races toward the upper right," states the quiltmaker in her vivid description of this piece. Dramatic as the optical effect of this quilt is, it is equally as impressive in its unusual construction. The quiltmaker first created a circular piece through the use of padded strip-piecing, then cut the circle into sections and rotated them into new orientations "to create depth and movement." Between the strips of color, carefully arranged by hue, are tiny strips of contrast fabric as narrow as piping. The quiltmaker draws on the philosophy of Carl Jung to describe her quilt: "The circle as a symbol of wholeness is the 'ouroboros' from which we break out as children on our paths to adulthood. Ideally, we circumambulate around our personal centre until, with maturity, we again experience the all-encompassing wholeness of the circle over again, this time consciously. It is my hope to be able to express this circular journey with fabric, creating mood and tension by pushing colour, texture, and technique to their unknown limits." A trained sculptor, the quiltmaker taught herself to quilt. She usually worked with welded steel in her sculpture, but would occasionally work with fabric for a change of pace ". . . but it was frowned on by my painter husband at the time. Now I work with fabric exclusively."

18. *Reflections and Illusions III* by Marilyn Stothers, Winnipeg, Manitoba, Canada. 1985. 49″ x 49″. Cotton and poly-cotton fabrics. Machine-pieced, machine- and hand-quilted. This is the designer's third quilt in a series that uses the theme of circles within squares with a dimensional perspective. "A great deal can be learned from exploring one design," she explains, "by working through a series of related shapes but in varying colours, fabrics, dimensions, sizes, and juxtapositions. The finished work may be very similar to, or may be very different from, the preceding work. It is important for a quilt artist to stretch the mind as well as try various techniques," she adds. Over the past two years, she has developed a new method of assembling fabric called *curved strip-piecing* and has received a government grant for continued work in this area. Although used like conventional straight strip-piecing, the new method requires fabric strips to be cut with wavy or curving edges before being joined to create new fabric strips from which shapes are then cut and reassembled. "The curved strip-piecing technique contributes to more fluid, softened lines within shapes, giving an optical and textural effect," she points out. The effect of the new method is best seen in the pastel background in this particular quilt. The reverse side of the quilt features an entirely different design, showing still another use for the curved strip-piecing.

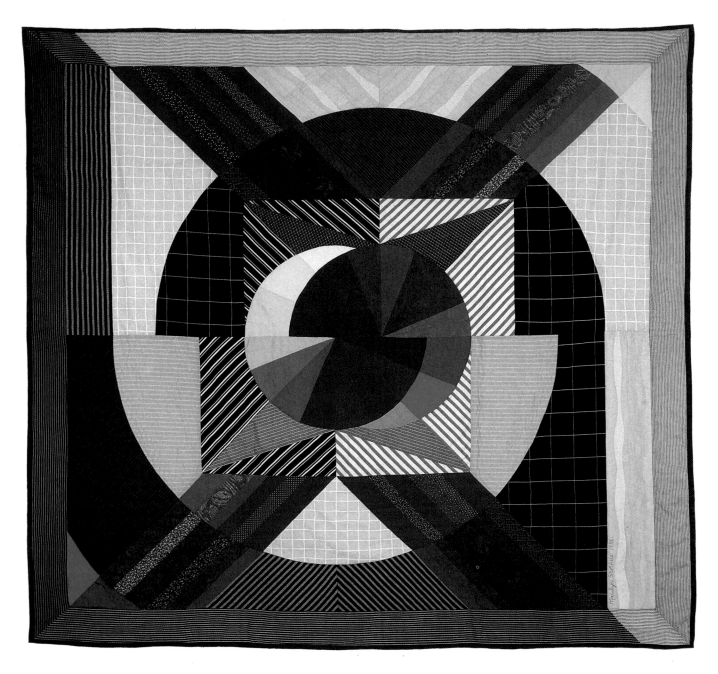

19. *Reflections and Illusions IV* by Marilyn Stothers, Winnipeg, Manitoba, Canada. 1986. 55″ x 58″. Cotton, poly-cotton, brocade fabrics, cotton flannelette batting. Machine-pieced, machine-quilted, hand-quilted. Fourth in a series, this quilt achieves an asymmetrical effect by having one half of the design mathematically shifted to free the concept. Intense colors are used in this piece, in which the circles and squares are less pronounced than in the other quilt from this series shown in figure 18. This quilt was also pieced by the unusual curved strip-piecing method originated by the quiltmaker.

20. *Curving Cubes II* by Marilyn Stothers, Winnipeg, Manitoba, Canada. 1985. 74″ x 74″. Cotton, poly-cotton fabrics. Machine-pieced, machine-quilted. The cube appears in succession behind a grid; sometimes the grid is flat, other times it is dimensional. The use of the triangle shapes, which change in color, add to the feeling of movement. This quilt is the second in a sculptural series that utilizes many shapes "to tease the eye of the viewer." The reverse side of the quilt is a completely different design in which the cube reappears.

21. *Six- and Ten-Pointed Stars* by Beatriz Castro, Santiago, Chile. 1983. 78″ x 98″. Cotton fabrics, polyester batting. Machine-pieced, machine-quilted. A striking medallion design executed in colors typical of the native textiles of Chile, this quilt represents an ambitious piecing project based on unusual, seldom-seen ten-pointed stars. These are basically constructed around a combination of interlocking six-pointed stars, but the quilt presents a much more complicated effect. "My design was inspired by a braided belt of the Cabuza style (Andean culture) found on archaeological sites of northern Chile," explains the quiltmaker. She first found a drawing of the Cabuza belt in an anthropological publication edited by the University of Tarapacá in Arica, Chile. It was made in the pre-Inca period when textile forms and decorations were highly developed. "The original colors used in the design were very brilliant," explains the quiltmaker. "The colors I used are different, but I tried to maintain the contrast between the different threads of the braid so that the different designs—the six- and ten-pointed stars—can be seen." The quiltmaker first saw a patchwork quilt in 1977 in the home of an American friend who was living in Santiago. She taught herself to quilt from books and magazines, and later made two separate trips to the United States to study special techniques.

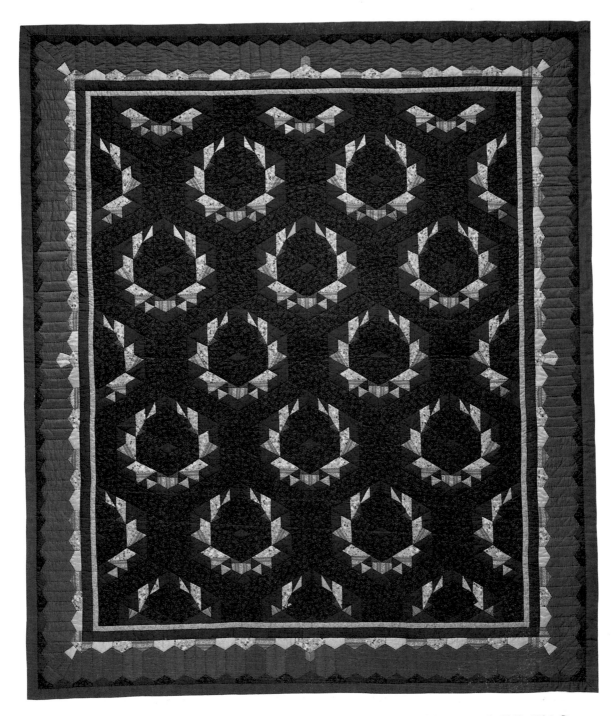

22. *Bruderkransen* by Anne Marie Harrison and the Patchwork Fonden, Holbaek, Denmark. 1983–1984. Cotton and poly-cotton fabrics. Hand-pieced and hand-quilted. Stylized wreaths of whimsical, pieced flowers spark the deep midnight blue of this quilt. A group project of the Patchwork Fonden, the piece was designed by Anne Marie Harrison, chairman of the foundation. The unusual border treatment provides an effective frame for the geometric design. The illusion of curves is created entirely by piecing straight edges together in a contemporary answer to the age-old challenge of creating rounded forms without using curved pieces. "Modern Danes, who pride themselves on their very personal style in design and home furnishings, find reproducing the old patchwork patterns a little unsatisfactory and seek a more contemporary form of creativity in their work," explains the designer. The quilt is made entirely by hand. "I never use the machine, as I have found that properly planned needlework is far more relaxing than the use of machine-sewing, and as the amount of relaxation is part of the value of a patchwork quilt, I do not wish to change. I have nevertheless been able to cut tedious and repetitive work in a number of ways. Members of the Patchwork Fonden have found that our work methods facilitate collective work without losing essential accuracy and quality; more and more students and members are discovering the social enjoyment hidden in collective undertakings."

23. *Victoria and Albert* by Lotte Jacobsen, Roskilde, Denmark. 1982. 85″ x 59″. Cotton fabrics, polyester batting. Hand-pieced, hand-quilted. "I made this quilt because I fell in love with an eighteenth-century bedcurtain in the Victoria and Albert Museum in London," says the quiltmaker who produced this beautifully colored clamshell design. The antique bedcurtains, a section of which is shown in the English book *Patchwork & Appliqué*, reflect early use of the traditional clamshell design constructed by the English paper-piecing method. The quiltmaker duplicated this method by basting fabric over egg-shaped paper templates to create each individual shell, and then hand-stitching the shells together to form the overall design. Each large section contains twenty-five shells framed by a dark green row to form diamond shapes. The quiltmaker selected the colors "to make it look Victorian." To achieve the complex surface design, she used many different European prints, plus a few American ones. Self-taught, she was introduced to quilting when she purchased a copy of *America's Quilts and Coverlets* in a book sale and "discovered that quilting is more than joining hexagons."

24. *Räumliche Wand* by Elrid Metzkes, East Berlin. 1985. 250 x 200 cm (94¹¹/₁₆″ x 75¾″). Silk fabrics. Pieced. Demonstrating a mastery of space and dimension, this quiltmaker, who works in the Deutsche Demokratische Republik, has elevated the basic Tumbling Blocks design to an abstract, optical illusion. Each face of the basic block has been pieced in one of three variations—bars, a checkerboard, or a framed diamond with its center divided into two triangles. Through the manipulation of these three surfaces, she produces the stunning illusion of a mysterious city of private rooms. Some of the rooms, like some people's lives, are entirely open to public view, others carefully closed off for privacy. Still other "rooms" reveal only tantalizing glimpses of space, just as most lives present two faces, the public and the private. Initially trained as a Gobelin weaver, the quiltmaker received her first impression of quilting in 1978, when she saw a small old patchwork quilt in a German country museum. "This technique showed me the way to ornamental clarity without using the weaving loom. From then on, for me, the loom was only for pictorial carpets," says the artist. All of her quilts are made of hand-dyed natural raw silk, both by choice and by necessity. "I don't want to copy old patchwork, so I turn myself toward the possibilities that live in the textures and muted glow of dyed silk."

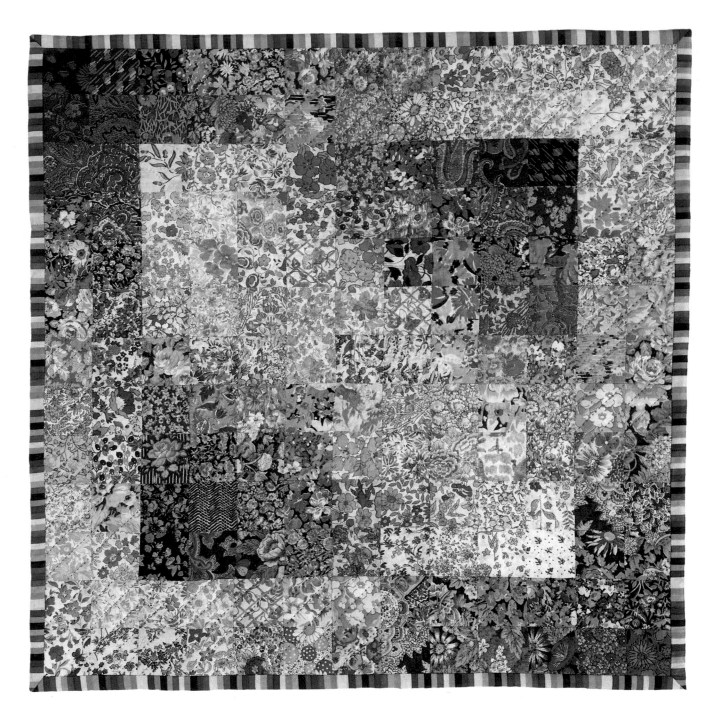

25. *Colourwash Framed I* by Deirdre Amsden, Cambridge, England. 1985. 20½″ x 20½″. Cotton fabrics, cotton batting. Machine-pieced, hand-quilted. Inspired by painting exercises using watercolors, the quiltmaker has refined her technique of creating the subtle movement of light and shadow with complex prints by working with 1½″ squares of cotton lawn to create the meticulous wall quilts illustrated here and in the following illustration. As she explains, "The arrangement of the squares does not follow a set pattern. Sometimes my initial idea is carried out quite easily, whereas at other times there is a tremendous struggle and the pieces just will not be arranged. Sometimes they almost seem to arrange themselves during or after several days of struggling. I use a reducing glass to check the arrangement all the time."

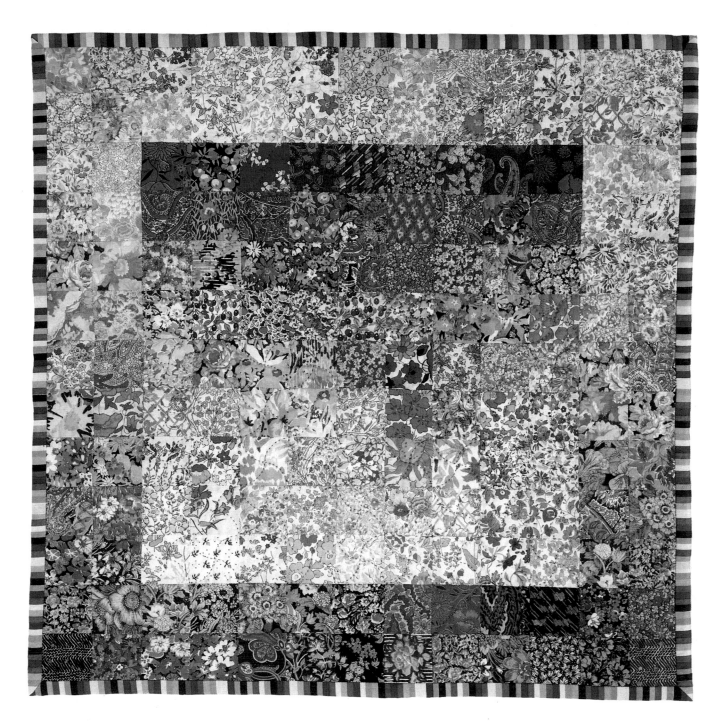

26. *Colourwash Framed II* by Deirdre Amsden, Cambridge, England. 1985. 20½″ x 20½″. Cotton fabrics, cotton batting. Machine-pieced, hand-quilted. The pair of quilts shown here and on the previous page is part of her second series of small hangings and was commissioned for a School Loan Scheme. They are constructed from Tana lawn, made by Liberty of London, a particularly fine, soft cotton that features delicate, muted prints. American quilters are often frustrated in using this English lawn because of the difficulty in blending prints; that a solution is possible is obvious here, where a close comparison might be made to an unusually sophisticated Depression-era scrap quilt. The sinuous curves of the quilting in the central blocks are part of a deliberate plan to diffuse the different prints so as to appear to be a whole piece of cloth. To that end, the seams of the patchwork are also pressed open. "I enjoy being able to do something in cloth that I was never able to master with watercolour paints," comments the quiltmaker.

27. *Persian Poppies* by Jenny Bardwell, Norwich, Norfolk, England. 1984. 95″ x 87″. Cotton fabrics, polyester batting. Machine-pieced, hand-appliquéd, hand-quilted. Striving to create a quilt that closely resembles the look of a Persian carpet, the quiltmaker adapted the traditional Ruby McKim poppy design and bordered it with an intricate star pattern planned to resemble Islamic tiles. The border design represents a joint effort between the quiltmaker and her draftsman husband, Leslie, who "calculated how many pieces would be needed for the border but wouldn't tell me . . . because he knew I'd think twice about embarking on it if I realized there were going to be more pieces in the border than in the main part of the quilt! I started this quilt when my second child, a daughter, was two months old. The project became an increasingly important part of my life: it was a symbol that I was still able to create something lasting and hopefully meaningful amongst the nappies, night feeds, tantrums from my twenty-month-old, and general chaos. I even found myself creeping downstairs to work on the quilt after Emily's 4 A.M. feed! I could never have made the quilt without Leslie's love, help, and support. He helped draft the borders, cut out quite a lot of the border pieces for me, and often took the children out at weekends so I could get on with the quilt. If the quilt is successful, it's his success, too—and we both love to sleep under it!"

28. *Memories of Suffolk* by Jacqueline R. Claiborne, Wivenhoe, Essex, England. 1984. 63″ x 59″. Cotton fabrics. Hand-pieced, hand-appliquéd, embroidered, dyed, hand-quilted. This creation, the quiltmaker's first hand-quilted piece, epitomizes "beginner's luck," as it won the Best of Show award at its very first competition. In studying this rendition of three young girls reading on the village green with the sun lighting the fields, the viewer is transported back in time to the halcyon days of childhood in a small English village. It clearly demonstrates a mastery of needlework skills, despite the quiltmaker's being a novice in quilting. "I dyed some of the fabric to get the right greens," she explains. "I wanted this quilt to look like a painting, and after eight months of work, I was satisfied that I had achieved my objective." The dreamy expressions on the three girls' faces and the meticulous detailing of the village in the background were accomplished with embroidery. The quilting design conveys the gentle curves of the land and the texture of the leaves and grass just as explicitly as the embroidered details on the schoolgirls' garments. The quiltmaker was intrigued by quilting while she lived for a time in the United States in the late 1970s. She is entirely self-taught.

29. *Royal Wedding* by Gillian Clarke, Moseley, Birmingham, England. 1983. 112″ x 112″. Cotton and poly-cotton fabrics, polyester batting. Hand-appliquéd, pieced, hand-quilted. A framed medallion quilt made to commemorate the marriage of Prince Charles and Lady Diana Spencer, this lively piece reflects both traditional and contemporary influences. The design incorporates traditional wedding patterns—the complete Bridal Wreath in the center and portions appearing in the corner blocks, and Steps to the Altar—along with design elements representing the monarchy. Parts of the quilt were cut out while the quiltmaker watched the royal wedding on television in 1981; more than two years were required to complete the quilt. As the quiltmaker explains, "Tudor Roses represent the Welsh family which came to the English throne in 1485, and Oak Leaves represent the oak tree in which Charles II hid after his defeat at the Battle of Worcester in 1651. The corner symbols are (clockwise from lower left) daffodils representing Wales, the Spencer coat of arms, the Prince of Wales' feathers, and a Cornish chough (the Prince of Wales is also Duke of Cornwall). The framed medallion commemorative quilt has a long tradition in Britain, and the outermost border of this quilt is copied from one made to record the Duke of Wellington's victory at Vitoria in 1813." This detailed, precisely planned quilt combining historical symbolism and romance is the work of a self-taught stitcher who began as "a patchworker, using scraps left over from dressmaking. Quilting followed, but I still tend to emphasize the patchwork design."

30. *Oxfam* by Gillian Clarke, Moseley, Birmingham, England. 1984. 64″ x 62″. Cotton and poly-cotton fabrics, polyester batting. Hand-appliquéd, pieced, hand-quilted. An original design reflecting Islamic ideas and mysticism, this quilt was inspired by the British charity, Oxfam, dedicated to worldwide relief of poverty and distress. The quiltmaker works regularly as a volunteer in a local Oxfam shop, where the quilt was displayed during a community festival in 1984. "We won third prize in the window dressing competition," she reports, "but to my chagrin, the quilt was described as a collage in the local paper!" The design themes predominant in the quilt are water, life, and mutual support. The entwined Tree of Life in the center shelters two smaller, younger trees. Two overturned pots in the inner corners pour out streams of water to nourish fruit trees, vines, vegetables, and a furrowed field where young plants grow. "The water runs down to a storage pond for future use, providing a home for fish, and sustaining trees on its banks. At the top are the fruits of harvest, and else-where, reminders of goods from overseas—baskets, birds drawn from Indian embroidery, and a pattern adapted from Indian inlaid work," explains the quiltmaker.

31. *Mallards* by Pamela A. Cross, London, England. 1984. 36″ x 48″. Hand-appliquéd, machine-pieced, hand-quilted. Inspired by a scale drawing in the Decoy House of Vermont's Shelburne Museum, this quilt is a tribute to both the mallards on Lake Winnipesaukee in New Hampshire and Britain's most common duck. The background was first pieced by machine; the mallards were then hand-appliquéd in their swimming positions. Patterns for the ducks were adapted from actual plans for wooden decoys. As the quiltmaker explains, "I found myself fascinated by decoys, which we don't see in England. My decoys are simply constructed in fabric rather than wood." The mallards also have a personal significance for her and for the American friends for whom the quilt was created as a gift. "When I stayed with my friends every summer at their home on the lake, the mallards would come up to be hand-fed. Then I stayed away for six years, and the mallards disappeared. They didn't return until the exact day I returned to the lake." The water is quilted in designs that reflect the natural ripples caused by the birds' movement and by the small whirlpool.

32. *Washburn* by Sheila Wells, Newbury, Berkshire, England. 1984. 36″ x 48″. Cotton and poly-cotton fabrics. Machine-pieced, hand-appliquéd, dyed, batiked, hand-quilted. "I wanted to give my daughter something to keep that would bring back memories," explains the quiltmaker about her design, made for a twenty-first birthday. "We have spent many happy family holidays in this beautiful part of England, and my daughter has taken part in white-water canoe races on the River Washburn." The quilt depicts the River Washburn in autumn through a combination of strip-piecing and hand-appliqué. "The Washburn is a fast-flowing Yorkshire river running through a deep wooded valley with typical dry-stone walls that separate it from the moorlands and fells." After making a full-size drawing of the quilt, based on photographs taken by her husband, the quilter marked the strip shapes directly on the drawing to use as a guide. To capture the subtleties of the woodland scene, she used many different scraps; some were batiked to look like rocks and others were home-dyed for special effects.

33. *Rainbow Lattice* by Sheila Wells. Newbury, Berkshire, England. Machine-pieced, hand-quilted. Based on a lattice design found in a book about geometry in Arabian art, strip-piecing has been used by the quiltmaker to elaborate upon that design. Her quilt has been featured in Valerie Campbell-Harding's book, *Strip Patchwork*, published in England. The gradations of color behind the interwoven lattice add a fascinating dimension to this quilt.

34. *Les Champs de Blé au Cachemire* by Soizik Labbens, Paris, France. 1984. 80″ x 80″. Cotton fabrics. Hand- and machine-pieced, hand-quilted. *Wheatfields in Cashmere* was created as a commissioned piece for a museum, to be used as the counterpoint for a planned exhibit of nineteenth-century antique paisleys. Since the museum specified that the piece was to be made of modern fabrics, the quiltmaker selected a fabric from Provence, in the south of France, for the center and combined this with green chintz and contemporary paisleys for the rest of the quilt. "This quilt certainly reflects something of my country," says the quiltmaker. "Indeed, this is quite French!" The heavily patterned fabrics add richness and depth to this piece. The large corner triangles of paisley balance the delicate design of the center fabric, which has been heavily quilted for a contrasting texture. The central design lent its name to the quilt. The quiltmaker is internationally known for her contemporary quilts. She teaches quilting in France and other European countries, as well as the United States, and has had her work accepted for exhibit in Quilt National and other important exhibitions in the United States and Europe. She discovered traditional patchwork at the first French exhibit of antique American quilts held in 1972 at the Musée des Arts Decoratifs in Paris. In 1974 she learned quilting from Sophie T. Campbell (see following page) at Le Rouvray, a Paris quilt shop.

35. *The Paris Presentation Quilt* by Le Patchwork Club de France, Paris, France. 1982. 96″ x 96″. Cotton and poly-cotton fabrics. Hand-pieced and hand-quilted. Following in the time-honored tradition of the American quilting bee, twenty-eight Frenchwomen gathered together in Paris to create this sampler quilt composed of ninety-eight different traditional designs. They worked under the direction of American quilter Sophie T. Campbell, who describes this historic quilt, the first of its kind to be made by Frenchwomen working in a group: "Le Patchwork Club de France was initiated from a need expressed to me by several of my students, the very same need that historically brought American women together in the quilting bee: the universal need of women to share their skills and friendship, to sympathize with each other, and to sew and compete, thereby obtaining a bit of recognition and appreciation." Participants in the making of *The Paris Presentation Quilt*: Jocelyne Assoun, Cheryl Audier, Françoise Blouzon, Marguerite Bonnet, Marie Bouet, Jocelyne Brice, Sophie T. Campbell, Janine Ciuntu, Françoise Courcenet, Colette Delesalle, Geneviève Doguet, Annette Dunod, Hélène Durand, Andrée Felix, Christine Gallot, Liliane Guerri, Yvonne Labadie, Marie Paule Mariani, Françoise Mercier, Martine Mosser, Luce Pauly, Jacqueline Pegorier, Cécile Pelpel, Jacqueline Perrusclet, Marguerite Peythieu, Elisabeth Rabault, Claudine Robert, Colette Tassou, Michele Thibault.

36. *Patience* by Mona Novotny Kouyioumtzis, Athens, Greece. 1984. 245 x 210 cm (92¹³/₁₆″ x 79½″). Cotton fabric, polyester batting. Embroidered, hand-quilted. "The quality and beauty we get from life depend on the patience and love we put into living," states this quiltmaker. "When I started the 'Patience Quilt' early in 1980, I was a very impatient person, so the quilt was my way of learning patience. The rules I worked with were very simple. First, I set no time limit on finishing the quilt. Second, I never worked on it unless I could relax and care about what I was doing. In the summer of 1984, after hundreds of hours of work, I finished the quilt. I think of it as a sort of diploma, which shows I 'graduated' a much more patient person!" The embroidery designs for this quilt were adapted from a series of eighteenth- and nineteenth-century cross-stitch designs from Argyrokastrom, Greece, which have been on display at the Benaki Museum in Athens. The designs include flowers, trees, and animals embroidered in seven colors. "Quilts are rarely made in Greece now, but there is a tradition of quilting as a craft and art form," she explains. Two types of Greek "quilts" exist. One consists of two layers of solid-color fabric over batting, quilted in straight lines. The second type contains two fabric panels sewn together, with a large hole in one panel. This hole is used like a pocket into which a heavy blanket or flokati rug can be placed.

37. *Memory Without End* by Kitty van Rhijn-Boersema, Odijk, Holland. 1983. 95 x 85 cm (36″ x 32″). Cotton fabrics. Pieced, hand-quilted. Blue and white has been a popular Dutch color combination since before the eighteenth century. Blue-and-white tiles and Delft china were synonymous with Holland for centuries, along with blue-and-white printed fabrics. "The color blue has specific Dutch significance, and some of the fabrics used in this piece are also used in the women's dresses of the fisherman's village of Spakenburg," explains the quiltmaker. The blue prints in this quilt resemble the blue-and-white wax-resist prints widely used in Europe during the eighteenth century. The wax-resist technique is also known as batik, commonly used in the Dutch East Indies, now Indonesia, and the Dutch West Indies. Batik fabrics were brought back to Holland as trade goods by the Dutch trading companies. The oval compass of this quilt was designed for the quilter by Hanne de Koning. A French Soleiado print has been used for the border of this piece. Suffering from low spirits while her husband was abroad, this Dutch quilter turned to patchwork: "It was Sunday, and Ewijckshoeve introduced the new season's patchwork and quilting courses. Seeing the beautiful and colorful quilts, I decided to make one myself and I felt happy again," she recalls.

38. *Catharina's Compass* by Rina Schouten-Vergunst, Driebergen, Holland. 1983. 300 x 130 cm (113 ¹¹/₁₆″ x 49¼″). Cotton fabrics. Pieced, hand-quilted. Glowing pastels seem to shimmer in a visual illusion created by the intricate piecing of this quilt, a variation of a traditional Mariner's Compass pattern. The pink geometric form that encircles the large compass is an unusual departure from the traditional, as is the inner circular row of lavender and purple triangles. "I received some chintz fabrics as a present from a quilting friend," explains the quiltmaker in discussing her color choices. "The radiant colors fascinated me, and I decided that they should be the needles of a compass, a huge compass." She has repeated the basic compass design at the top and bottom of this piece and reversed the color combinations, which creates a different optical effect. A retired teacher at a school of domestic economics, she "kept my needles and thread busy" and soon decided that "piecing and quilting is a life necessity." The Compass is a particularly appropriate design for a Dutch quilt because of the age-old economic relationship Holland has had with the sea. Dutch seamen and captains are as active in world shipping today as they were 300 years ago, and the compass still plays an important navigational role.

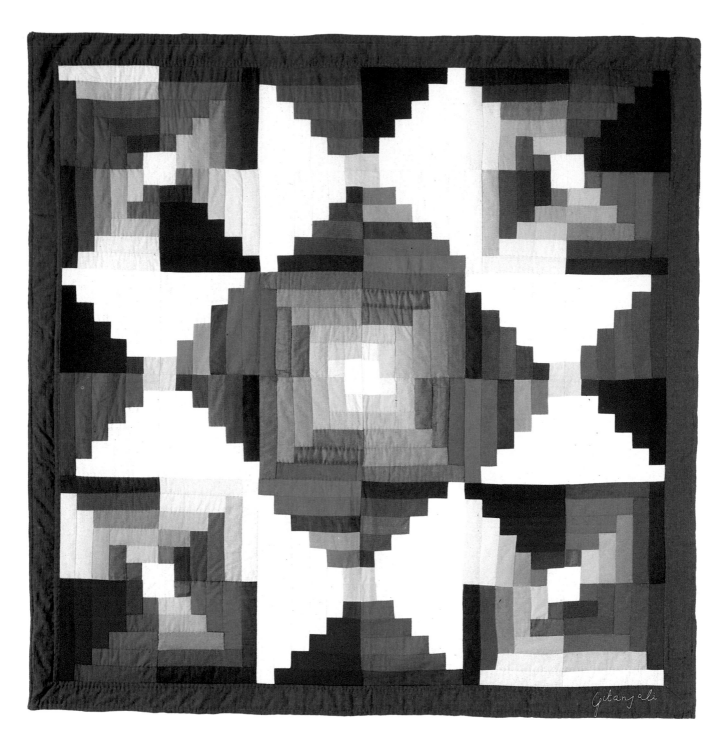

39. *Hope* by Geeta Khandelwal, Bombay, Maharashtra, India. Cotton fabrics. Pieced, quilted. Thirty different shades have been used to produce this variation of the traditional Log Cabin pattern, in which the blocks have been arranged to form a star. The design was intended to convey "youthful exuberance." Historically, certain types of quilts have been produced in the villages of India, particularly Gujarat and Rajasthan, and the quilt-maker has collected examples of original antique Indian quilts. However she herself turned to quilting as "the outcome of a bored, suffocated, and restricted housewife trying to save. I saved food, clothing, bits of wire, even threads, until I ended up with bags full of leftover materials, wires, plugs, etc. One day these sacks full of beautiful fabrics blossomed into patchwork designs." Today she designs and produces quilts as an export business, which her husband encouraged her to try after seeing the work of a professional quilter from the United States on display at the American Center in Bombay. From a love of handwork instilled in her by her mother who insisted she fill her free time with "chainstitching and embroidery to perfection," she has built a business that today involves forty other Indian women learning and working with her.

40. *Anniversary Quilt* by Margaret McClintock Slutz, Sumatra, Indonesia. Cotton fabrics. Pieced, hand-quilted. Fascinating, complex Javanese batiks in warm rusts and browns lift this traditional quilt far out of the ordinary. The lushly printed fabric of the pieced Lone Star provides a central focus, emphasized by four inner borders and an outer pieced border adapted from *Sentimental Journey*, as shown in *Quilter's Newsletter Magazine*. The pale peach border was hand-dyed using seedpods from a local tree called Kesumba. A dark outer border frames the whole. Design motifs from the fabrics used for the Lone Star were carefully arranged to form secondary designs within each diamond, using methods outlined in the *Lone Star Quilt Handbook*. Made as a celebration quilt to commemorate a special anniversary, this quilt will also serve as a reminder of life in Rumbai, an oil company camp in Sumatra, which is the largest island in Indonesia. "There is no quilting done by Sumatrans," reports the quiltmaker, a native Texan. "Instead they produce beautiful embroidery on the native dresses of western Sumatra, and in northern Sumatra there is a kind of weaving called ikat that is popular." Quilting in Sumatra is a challenge for the five or six American quilters living there: although unusual fabrics are plentiful, to buy batting requires a trip to Singapore.

41. *Galway Hookers* by Ann Fahy, Bushy Park, County Galway, Ireland. 1984. 67″ x 64″. Cotton and cotton-blend fabrics. Machine-pieced, hand-quilted. Galway Hookers are old Irish sailboats formerly used for trading in Galway Bay and around the west coast of Ireland. Today they are being lovingly restored and used for summer racing. The sharp, angular lines of the boats and their sails as they skim across the water are captured beautifully in this original design, which was made to celebrate the Quincentennial (500th anniversary) of the granting of a charter to Galway City. The quiltmaker, who learned to quilt when she "answered an ad for classes in a local paper," especially enjoys working with geometric forms. Here she began with an outline of a hooker and its reflection in the water, creating a simple block design that she repeated diagonally. The diagonal set formed still another pattern, which she has executed in the colors of the sea and sky. Her quilting designs repeat the lines of the sails, create a wave pattern for the sea, and emphasize a circular "cloud" pattern for the sky. The Corrib Quilters, a group that meets weekly in her home, provided assistance in piecing and quilting this design. Quilts in Ireland have traditionally meant whole-cloth quilts made of *bainin,* a fine white wool, and backed with red flannel; today, however, many Irish quilters are working with contemporary designs.

42. *Third Eye* by Evelyn Montague, Cork, Ireland. 1985. 66″ x 66″. Cotton fabrics. Machine-pieced, hand-quilted. A dodecahedron, or twelve-sided quilt, this original design was inspired by the *Passiflora* (passion-flower) growing in the quiltmaker's garden. However, the wall hanging "ended a far cry from what I originally intended," according to the designer. The flower is based on two sets of five petals, which defeated her mathematical ability until a painter friend suggested she stop concentrating on the object and look at its surroundings. "From then on, I was possessed," she says. The sections of the quilt were designed as she went along; each section had to harmonize with her previous efforts. She ended the design when it was possible to reintroduce the yellow of the center because she wanted an open effect. A Frenchwoman who married an Irish poet and moved from Paris to Ireland thirteen years ago, the quiltmaker holds dual nationality. "When I married and moved to Ireland, what had been a professional, active, and social life became an idle, solitary, and contemplative life," she explains. "My affections are equally divided between my two countries. That shows up in my quilt, because I realized as I progressed that more than I had originally planned went into this design—it had been in my head since my Paris years, a personal mandala. It also satisfied my urge to bridge the contradictions of my exile: I live in Ireland surrounded by intense natural beauty but scant man-made efforts, yet I come from France where the concept of 'you are what you create' runs deep."

43. *Flaming Drum* by Sanae Hattori, Yokohama City, Japan. 1985. Cotton and silk fabrics. Hand-appliquéd, hand-pieced, hand-quilted. A stunning visual concept, this quilt draws its strength from both the exciting design elements and the fascinating interplay of Japanese symbolism. The flames leap out into the night sky, filled with spinning stars, just as the rising sun, symbolized by the central chrysanthemum, splinters the dark with rays of light. White, for light and purity, represents the coming dawn. The drum itself is an ancient symbol of war, and in Oriental mythology, the use of red symbolizes the god of war. A variation of the traditional Tumbling Blocks pattern forms the sky full of stars. Vermilion red, a bright orange-red, captures the leaping flames and, at the same time, recalls the royal use of this color in early Japan. Gold thread has been used to outline and quilt certain sections of the quilt. The quiltmaker, author of *The Quilt Japan*, is professionally trained in art and traditional Japanese embroidery. Although patchwork is an ancient technique in Japan, quilting other than *sashiko* was seldom seen until after World War II, when the American presence in postwar Japan introduced many elements of Western culture.

44. *Soaring Crane* by Sanae Hattori, Yokohama City, Japan. Cotton and silk fabrics. Hand-appliquéd, pieced, hand-quilted. Symbol of longevity and herald of eternity, the crane of Oriental legend is poised for flight to heaven. One ancient custom calls for a crane with outspread wings to be placed on the center of a coffin in a funeral procession so that the soul of the departed may ride to heaven on the back of the bird. The quiltmaker has bordered her creation with a contemporary adaptation of the traditional Flying Geese design, each border showing the geese flying in a different direction. The delicacy of the designer's work is most evident in the feathers, which are pieced, appliquéd, and quilted in detail.

45. *Weeping Cherry Branches* by Sanae Hattori, Yokohama City, Japan. Cotton and silk fabrics. Pieced, appliquéd, hand-quilted, embroidered. Delicate cherry blossoms of fabric so subtly hued that it could have been painted with watercolors are appliquéd onto a subdued gridwork print to produce a design that is both sophisticated and visionary. Striations of pastels are used for a raw silk border that seems to shimmer and float, almost like a gauze curtain over a rain-streaked window looking out onto a garden. The design was taken from a Kabuki costume used in the traditional *Musume Dojoje* dance.

46. *United States–Japan Friendship Quilt* by Japanese and American quilters, Tokyo, Japan, and New York City, U.S.A. Pieced, appliquéd, hand-quilted. Images of Japanese and American life and culture are depicted in many techniques, executed at many different skill levels, in this pilot project, a friendship-exchange quilt between the two nations. The quilt project was organized by Kei Kobayashi, a Japanese writer who now lives in New York, and involved students and teachers in both countries. Margory Frund's students in a quilting class at New York's New School of Social Research created the traditional square blocks for the project, and each student accompanied her block with a "pen pal" letter on fish-shaped paper. Setsuko Nakano's artcraft students of Bunka Fashion School in Tokyo finished the quilt with round blocks, each the image of a plate of Japanese food. The quilt has been displayed in New York at the Japan Air Lines Gallery as a friendship-exchange project, cosponsored by the airline and *SO-EN*, the largest fashion and life-style magazine in Japan. A similar quilt, *Fantasy of Dream Island*, contains thirty blocks made by Japanese quilters.

47. *Crane* by Hiroko Kawahito, Kagawa, Japan. 1985. 62″ x 62″. Cotton and silk fabrics. Hand-appliquéd, hand-quilted. Crane quilts in all their variations are the specialty of this quiltmaker, whose family business uses the Origami Crane as its symbol. Owners of a sake (Japanese rice wine) brewery, the family each year displays all of the designer's Crane quilts in the brewery at the annual open house when the year's new sake is celebrated and shared with the townspeople. Handwoven fabrics, cottons hand-dyed with indigo, and kimono silks were combined to produce this formal, stylized quilt. Some of the fabrics were found in the family's warehouse. The cranes' designs are taken from the art of origami, or paper-folding, and their whimsical placement adds a lively spirit to this otherwise stately piece. This quilt has been displayed at quilt exhibitions in the United States and Switzerland.

48. *Japanese Talisman* (*Noshi*) by Jill Liddell, Tokyo, Japan. 178 x 114 cm (67^{7}/₁₆″ x 43^{3}/₁₆″). Hand-appliquéd, hand-quilted. An elegant, formal design, this quilt depicts two recurring symbols of Japanese culture: the decorative ribbon and flying cranes. To the Japanese, presentation is as important as substance: gifts are presented with great ceremony, wrapped enticingly; tea is served in a ritual ceremony; food is presented thoughtfully and beautifully, arranged so that the plates themselves are examples of careful design. The ribbon bow, called *noshi* in Japanese and originally made from strips of dried abalone, blows gracefully in the wind, hovering in the sky like a kite. The flying cranes, symbols of longevity, are meticulously detailed and quilted realistically. The idiosyncratic placement of the cranes, with one shown flying off the quilt and another just flying into the design, adds both charm and visual interest to this piece. The background of the quilt is intricately quilted with two different fill-in designs, one of which is the tortoiseshell design, another symbol of long life. "The designs for this quilt were adapted from traditional Japanese kimonos that I saw in museum collections," the quiltmaker explains. A British woman living in Japan, she is writing a book on Japanese quilts that will be published in English.

49. *Spring Celebration* by Emi Masaoka, Tokyo, Japan. 1981. 81″ x 81″. Cotton and silk fabrics. Hand-pieced, hand-quilted. This is the first original quilt featuring Japanese designs made by this young quiltmaker. She was only twenty-three when she made the quilt and is one of the youngest quilters working in Japan. She has chosen to work with a dramatic palette, which might be expected from a city girl from old Tokyo: sharp, brilliant splashes of color against a somber, deep blue background. The design takes its charm from a combination of several different patterns, including the traditional Fan and the Chevron. The indigo background is quilted with *sashiko* designs, traditional Japanese quilting in white thread on a dark surface. The quilt, a distinct departure from the traditional, owes its creation to the fact that the quiltmaker was tired of piecing the same blocks over and over again and decided she would have more design freedom if she emphasized Japanese motifs, such as the sashiko stitching designs. She has used Japanese cotton sheeting, *yukata* fabrics, and textiles taken from a girl's kimono for use in the pieced work.

50. *Kagome (Basketwork)* by Ruri Miyamoto, Japan. 1984. 86″ x 59″. Cotton fabrics. Hand-pieced, hand-quilted. Based on traditional Japanese basketry, this quilt also draws on traditional textile and ornamental design for its inspiration. The simplicity of the original pieced design was deliberately planned to show off the many valuable antique fabric scraps the quiltmaker had collected. Although the basic design remains the same throughout the quilt, the subtle variation in intensity in the handwoven indigos used for the blue background creates a shaded effect. The center of each block showcases scraps of unusual Oriental fabrics: Japanese batiks as well as antique *aizome* fabrics, which are stenciled indigos. Japanese stitchers cherish even worn scraps of antique fabrics that are important in the history of textiles in that country; the women collect these scraps and proudly work them into contemporary designs.

51. *Peony* by Takako Morohashi, Tokyo, Japan. 1983. 67″ x 62″. Cotton fabrics. Trapunto, hand-quilted. Antique handwoven indigo, hand-painted with white peonies and pale leaves, was resurrected from a junk shop to be given a new life in this stunning Oriental quilt. The decorated fabric was formerly used to cover wedding furniture, an old tradition among wealthy Japanese families. The quiltmaker, proud of salvaging the treasured fabric, which was sold to her as a scrap, stuffed each painted peony by hand so the flowers stand out in relief. She then quilted the design intricately with traditional Japanese designs. The peony, as a symbol of good fortune is a favorite flower of the Chinese, and the flowing, beautifully balanced arrangement of the blossoms painted on this fabric is typically Chinese. However, the peony is also cherished by the Japanese as a harbinger of spring, just as the lotus represents summer, the chrysanthemum fall, and the plum blossom winter. The indigo fabric used as the background of this quilt was handwoven on a narrow loom, and the narrow vertical panels were seamed together by hand. This fabric is close kin to the ubiquitous American blue-jean denim. In early Japan, indigo blue was the only color commoners could afford to use because the dye could be produced from the easily grown plant. Sensing that the quilt is now living "a life of its own," the quiltmaker feels that "it is not really mine anymore, even though it still belongs to me," a somewhat wistful sentiment often shared by other artists.

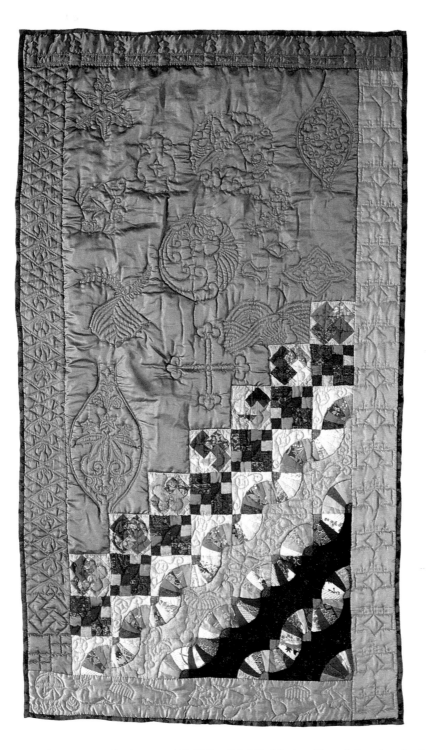

52. *Kyoto* by Hiroko Nakamura, Aichi, Japan. 1982. 78″ x 43″. Silk fabrics. Pieced, hand-quilted. Inspired by the traditional beauty of the old Japanese capital, Kyoto, this heavily quilted silk quilt also contains design elements borrowed from the costumes of geisha girls and temple ornaments. The quiltmaker has been designing predominantly Japanese quilts for more than five years; this piece is one of her early creations. She has used kimono silks in the patchwork and counterpane areas. Each border of the quilt is stitched in a different, elaborate pattern, and Japanese designs are quilted into the green silk. The patchwork section of the piece is ingeniously designed to derive maximum impact from basically simple pieced patterns: Card Trick, Four Patch, and Fan. It is the placement and juxtaposition of these basic designs that create such a complex effect, emphasized by the unusual color combinations.

53. *Antique Sashiko Jacket*, Takae Onoyama, owner, Tokyo, Japan. Cotton fabric. Hand-quilted. *Sashiko* quilting is an ancient tradition in Japan, and a fine example is seen in this nineteenth-century man's coat made of indigo-dyed handwoven cotton in the Hokuriku region of Japan. *Sashiko* is a simple running stitch always executed in white thread on a dark background, usually the indigo blue that was all the Japanese commoner was allowed to wear. The designs are always geometric, employing both straight lines and elaborate curves, and often resemble traditional American quilting patterns. Emphasis is placed on small, even stitches that create a surface design on the coarsely woven cotton, which is sometimes printed or stenciled to create a pattern. The effect of so much heavy quilting is to add significant weight to the garments and to make the reverse side of sashiko as fascinating as the front. The owner of this piece, an advanced collector of antique sashiko garments, has lent pieces from her collection for exhibitions in both Europe and the United States. Other garments in her collection include a nineteenth-century fireman's jacket that features extraordinarily heavy quilting to protect its wearer from the flames and a *nijiri*, an unusual 1870s quilted back protector used to cushion the weight of a loaded basket carried on the wearer's back. The collector is owner of Quilt House Yama in Tokyo.

54. *Kamon Sampler* by Yukiko Saito, Saitama, Japan. 1981. 103″ x 63″. Cotton and silk fabrics. Hand-pieced, hand-appliquéd, hand-quilted. *Kamon*s are Japanese family crests used on ceremonial occasions that frequently appear in Japanese quilting designs. Highly stylized motifs usually enclosed within a circle or other geometric form, kamons came to be used as family emblems as early as the sixteenth century. The crests are constructed using a variety of techniques, including reverse appliqué, stained-glass appliqué, and blind-stitch appliqué. The execution of these techniques indicates a mastery of appliqué, which reflects its highly developed state as an art form in the Orient. The background has been double quilted with two different designs and techniques. Japanese Blue Wave quilting, an overlapping curved design, is intersected with evenly spaced straight lines of *sashiko* quilting in contrasting, colored thread. The intriguing lattice sashing has been hand-pieced with smaller segments of the same fabrics that are repeated in the border framing this unusual quilt. Modern kamons are most often seen as embellishments on kimonos. The formality of a kimono can be judged by the number of kamons worn—a five-kamon kimono is the height of formality—as well as the fabric used in the construction of the garment. In addition, kamons are often used as family emblems on tombstones for old Japanese families.

55. *Game of Shells* by Masako Satoh, Japan. 1983. 67″ x 34″. Cotton, silk, and wool fabrics. Hand-pieced. Working with the traditional clamshell pattern, used for centuries to create patchwork, the quiltmaker set out "to make a real scrap quilt, like an old American scrap quilt only with Japanese fabrics." Her quilt is based on the early English method of constructing patchwork, which requires a paper template as the basis for every piece of fabric. "Some precious antique scraps are reinforced with a lining because they are 'tired,'" she adds. The extraordinary variety of the fabrics she has blended in this piece make it a scrapbook of antique Japanese textiles. Included are scraps of *aizome* stenciled fabrics, indigo checks and stripes, ikat weaves, Japanese batiks, kimono silks, handkerchiefs, and kimono wools, among others. The finished piece was intended to resemble the oblong balance of a quilted Japanese scroll, and the precise placement of light fabrics on the left edge and in a gentle curve is intended to enhance that effect.

56. *Sakura Fuji* (*Cherry Blossom and Wisteria*) by Keiko Yoshida, Tokyo, Japan. 1983. 78″ x 78″. Cotton and silk fabrics. Hand-pieced, hand-appliquéd, hand-quilted. Visually stunning, this quilt juxtaposes the delicacy of the floral designs against the stark contrast of the moonlight setting to produce an intriguing effect that almost echoes a Kabuki stage setting for traditional Japanese drama. The quilt is designed around a center patch of "moonlight," created by piecing small squares of monochromatic fabrics together in the traditional Postage Stamp design repeated at the edge of the "garden." The quiltmaker, a flower lover who grows, arranges, and sketches the flowers in her garden, produced many meticulous drawings of the blossoms before she found a pleasing pattern for the flower shapes. Luckily, her subject was close at hand: her favorite cherry trees at the entrance to her house. The cherry blossoms are an integral part of Japanese culture, and their blooming is a source of celebration each year. "Because the season is so fleeting, I decided to immortalize it forever," the quiltmaker says. "It took six months to complete the quilt. I started before the blossoms came out and finished after all the leaves had fallen." The design is a rendition of a favorite Japanese theme—flowers by moonlight—set in a Western manner resembling a medallion or the popular framed floral appliqués from the 1930s.

57. *Diamond Ring* by Margaret Corbett, Kaitaia, North Island, New Zealand. 1984. 96″ x 84″. Cotton and cotton blends on unbleached calico. Machine-pieced, hand-quilted, embroidered. A striking, original design, this wall quilt in green, beige, and rust features Crazy patchwork pieced to form a design of interlocking three-dimensional diamonds. Calicoes were first pieced together by hand, using the herringbone stitch, then cut apart using templates. The designs were then pieced together by machine and hand-quilted. The quiltmaker calls this method "patch and piece" and refers to it as "organized Crazy patchwork." "I found that by using the 'patch and piece' method I could have the best of both worlds—hand-sewn Crazy patchwork and a pieced design to give unity to randomness," she states. The quiltmaker is self-taught, learning initially from four quilting magazines she received as a gift. *Diamond Ring* marks a milestone in this quiltmaker's life. For three years she has been working alone in comparative isolation in the far north of New Zealand, before being invited to teach and exhibit at the Auckland National Quilt Symposium. The event was her first contact with quilters, and she treasured the invitation to join with other quilt lovers. She designed this celebration quilt to reflect the joy she felt at meeting and learning from them. "This design of linked diamonds symbolises for me the precious opportunity to meet fellow quilters from all over the country, to make new friends and to share with them the excitement of quilting."

58. *"Let Not the Sun Go Down…"* by Shirley Dixon, Wellington, New Zealand. 1985. Small wall quilt. Cotton fabrics. Hand-appliquéd, hand-quilted, soft sculpture. Witty and amusing, this is a highly original creation, the first in a proposed series of "quilt beds," where the quilt and the bed's occupants illustrate a well-known saying. The faces are attached to body-forms to give shape under the quilt, but the quiltmaker is emphatic in insisting that these are not dolls: "The whole bed is constructed and sewn as a piece for the wall or to be displayed on a table—it is not for little fingers to play with!" The faces are constructed out of what New Zealanders call "calico"—plain, off-white, unbleached cotton fabric. "The noses are separate pieces of fabric," explains the designer, "and the other features are quilted except for the coloured, stitched eyes. The hair is fine strips of fabric." Depicting the biblical verse found in Ephesians(4:26)—"Let not the sun go down upon your wrath"—this delightful piece shows the green hills for which New Zealand is famous as they appear at various times of day, from pale dawn to evening. The wide-awake couple lies rigid beneath the quilt, each person caught up in the disagreement, neither wanting to be the first to make peace. To capture such an emotional state in such small, hand-stitched faces is a challenge that reveals the true talent of this needle artist.

59. *Pukerua Bay Beach* by Marge Hurst, Pukerua Bay, Wellington, New Zealand. 1984. 40" x 47". Silk, cotton and poly-cotton fabrics. Machine-pieced, hand-quilted, free canvaswork embroidery. Drawing inspiration from photographs she had taken of Pukerua Bay Beach in her adopted homeland, the quiltmaker originally titled her work *Wish You Were Here* and dedicated it to all the friends she had left behind in the United States when she moved to New Zealand ten years earlier. Patchwork was part of her examination for the City and Guilds of London Embroidery Certificate, and the quiltmaker says she is "now an addict," after concentrating on other needlework for many years in her home state of Pennsylvania. Her reasoning for not taking up quilting sooner was that "...if I started [patchwork], nothing else would ever get done," an evaluation that she now admits was entirely correct! One assignment required for completion of the certificate was to produce a work that would encompass more than one needle art. This original work designed by the quiltmaker features a view of Pukerua Bay Beach and its surrounding houses and hills carried out in the following techniques: free canvas-work for the hills; machine-piecing for the houses and beach; strip-piecing for the sky; and quilting on silk for the sea.

60. *Evocation* by The Wednesday Night Group, Wellington, New Zealand. 1984. 90″ x 90″. Cotton and poly-cotton fabrics. Hand- and machine-pieced, stenciled, hand-quilted. For nineteen years, the seven members of The Wednesday Night Group have met to work together and encourage each other on individual stitchery projects. *Evocation* is their second group quilt. In 1974, one of the group taught herself American-style quilt-making from books, and her work inspired the rest of the women. At the time this particular quilt was being planned, Wellington's noteworthy Victorian Town Hall was in danger of being demolished. Since the group's aim was to blend techniques of American quiltmaking with a design from their New Zealand environment, tiles in the Town Hall's foyer and corridors became their inspiration. Small floral motifs found in the tiles were stenciled on fabric. The tile design is basically a central diamond medallion composed of four diamonds, each in turn composed of four Nine Patches that form a center star set off by the stenciled flowers. Intricate quilting echoes the floral designs, which in some section are encircled by double-quilted rings. An elaborate pieced inner border of blue and black triangles completes the tile effect. Members of The Wednesday Night Group are Shirley Dixon, Thelma Read, Flora Macdonald, Margaret Clarke, Peggy Nattrass, Adrienne Howard, and Frances Stone.

61. *Oil Production in Deep Waters* by Anne-Donia Bruun Hafskjold, Tiller, near Trondheim, Norway. 1984.
32" x 43". Silk and cotton fabrics. Machine-appliquéd, hand-quilted. Made as a surprise gift for her husband who
does research into oil production, this handsome wall quilt is the quiltmaker's first original design and her first
appliqué work. The piece was constructed by beginning at the bottom, and working upward in layered
appliqué similar to the way a Crazy quilt is made. The sea and the sky are both made of the same material,
"bought in 1936 for a very special dress!" They differ only in the quilting design used for the waves and the use
of the reverse side of the fabric for the sky. The subtle, understated contrast was chosen to mirror the way the
sky and the water blend together on a cloudy day. After the levels of the ocean floor, the sea and the sky were
appliquéd, and then the oil rig, platform, and pipeline were added. The pipeline was constructed from cords
twisted together to indicate the actual drilling motion. The flame was embroidered. "As a lover of all handi-
crafts, I fell in love with patchwork and quilting when I stayed in the U.S.A. from 1976 to 1978," the quilter
reports. She took a museum class in Port Jefferson, New York. She adds that there is no tradition of quilting in
Norway but knitting, crocheting, and embroidery have long been traditional needle arts.

62. *Grand Canyon* by Christine Berry, Glasgow, Lanarkshire, Scotland. 1984. 180 x 116 cm (68³/₁₆″ x 43¹⁵/₁₆″). Cotton and poly-cotton fabrics. Machine-pieced, hand-quilted. This quilt represents the colors and shapes found in the Grand Canyon as seen by the quiltmaker on a visit during her year's stay in the United States in 1973–1974. Layers of geologic strata provided the basic idea for a design project best suited to patchwork and quilting. "Although I originally intended to add surface stitchery, I eventually relied on the quilting to provide the texture," she says. That texture is indicated by varying amounts of quilting in the different stylized mountains and ridges of the canyon, and in the winding river that has carved its path between them. The rich hues of this masterpiece of nature also find their place in this quilt, with its purples, magentas, blues, rusts, apricots, and greens. Photographs and slides are important design sources for the quiltmaker's embroidery and quilting projects. Her initial interest in embroidery drew her to quilting as another needle art to explore. Viewing quilt exhibitions in the United States in 1980–1981 increased her interest in patchwork quilts, as opposed to the whole-cloth quilts typical of northeastern England and south Wales.

63. *The Secret Garden* by Jean M. Roberts, Currie, Midlothian, Scotland. 1984. 98″ x 72″. Cotton fabrics. Pieced, hand-appliquéd, hand-quilted. This quilt, with its deep, jewellike tones and complex English and American print fabrics, was made for the 1984 Thistle Quilters of Edinburgh exhibition, "Two Hundred Years of Patchwork and Quilting in Scotland," proof of the venerable tradition of this needle art in that country. The design is adapted from an illumination of the only surviving page of a double frontispiece of an Egyptian Qur'an, or Koran. This page was illustrated in the Mamluk and Mongol style and was produced sometime between the eighth and fourteenth century. Like the original frontispiece, this quilt has exploited geometric forms, with particular reference to the spider's web. The original colors used in the illustration were blue, the color of the infinite, and gold, symbol of the spirit, to which the quiltmaker has added green and red. "When I saw the Liberty print, it immediately reminded me of Frances Hodgson Burnett's lovely story, *The Secret Garden*. The illusion of secrecy was further enhanced by using the stained-glass technique, with the bias binding forming the 'walls' of the garden," the quiltmaker explains. Her daughter drafted the original rectangular design and enlarged it to fit a bed. Designs in the corners of the quilt are enlargements of the birds found in the Liberty print. The center design shows how a new circular design may be created by reassembling wedges of a single print.

64. *Floral Landscape* by Nina Lawrence, Westville, Natal, South Africa. 1983. 20″ x 30″. Appliquéd. A pictorial wall hanging in somber tones that form the hilly foreground and the overcast sky, this work is relieved by the gaiety of bright appliquéd flowers, some of which escape the confines of the piece's inner borders. The vivid colors of a spectacular sunset in warm golds and oranges, however, are the true focal point of this design in which the selection of prints was an important consideration that adds a complex tonality contributing to the overall effect. A quiltmaker who puts as many as forty-five hours into even her small works, Nina Lawrence is a frequent exhibitor at the Grassroots Gallery in Westville. She never sells her work, however, since family members claim it all. "I never have an excess," she notes.

65. *Embrasement* (*Conflagration*) by Maryline Collioud-Robert, Cortaillod, Switzerland. 1984. 167 x 114 cm (63¼″ x 43³/₁₆″). Cotton, poly-cotton, poly-wool, polyester, and silk fabrics, and polyester batting. Machine-pieced, hand-tied. This piece is part of a series in which the quiltmaker is concerned with the feelings generated by the whole surface of the work, rather than with individual blocks. "I like quilts to have a three-level impact on the viewer," she says. "The first glance must be the strongest; here a feeling of conflagration, strength, joy of living, love at first sight, anything coming strongly from the inside out. Then I like the block used to be evident. On closest view, I like the fabrics to be present. I always use some prints, to remind everyone that the quilt is also a textile object, not only a graphic statement." To emphasize the textile aspects of a design, she always pieces into the backing of a quilt odd fabrics that she has had on hand for some time, even though she could easily back the quilt with just one fabric. "My quilts are all 'cousins' this way," she says, and adds, "I like my quilts to look harmonious on the front, but I 'crazy' them on the back." In designing this quilt, she experimented with the possibilities of the triangular Log Cabin block. The dramatic shaded color combination creates a play of light across the surface that softens and blurs the edges of this sharply geometric quilt.

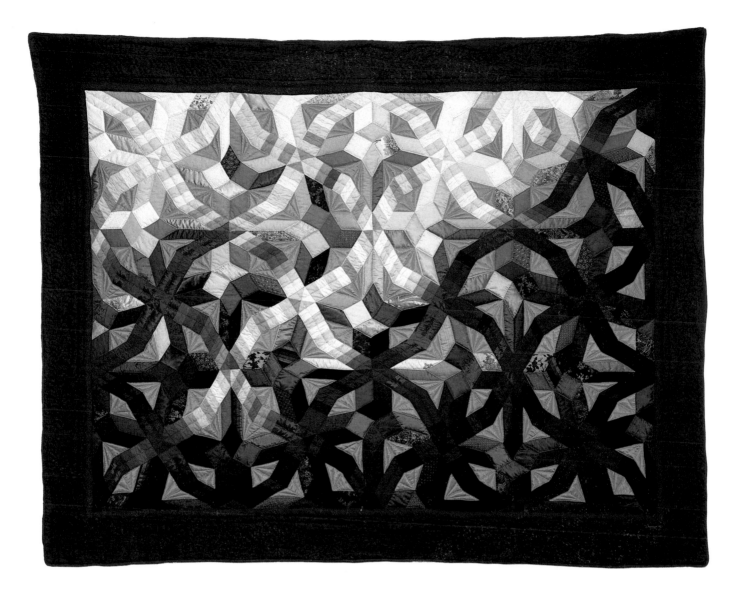

66. *Metropolitan* by Ursula Gerber-Senger, Männedorf, Switzerland. 1985. 73″ x 92″. Cotton, silk, satin, and velveteen fabrics, with polyester batting. Hand-pieced, hand-quilted. The intent of this quilt is to express the heart of a city with its roads, represented by the weaving of diagonal lines; its houses, shown in various blue tones with yellow accents; and the sky, represented in a brilliant blue satin. The snaking roads provide activity and movement that are contained by a narrow inner border and a wide outer one. The quilting on the sky is so heavily textured that it creates an image of clouds. The quiltmaker's basic concept for the quilt consists of the manipulation of a multitude of squares and rhombuses. After that, she says, "the rest is a game with light and shade." The artist discovered quilting while in Venezuela, where one of her American friend's bookshelves contained a paperback book on traditional quilts. "It was something new for me," she says.

67. *Sunset City* by Ursula Gerber-Senger, Männedorf, Switzerland. 1985. 67″ in circumference. Silk, cotton, and velveteen fabrics, polyester batting. Hand-pieced, machine-pieced, and hand-quilted. Again working with the basic square and rhomboid shapes, this time within an overall circular format, the quiltmaker's purpose was to convey a city removed from its setting and transposed into the middle of the setting sun. Strongly visual, the circular design presents a formidable challenge, but is an inspired choice to indicate both the ongoing, ceaseless activity of urban life and the whirling, seething orb of the sun itself.

68. *Berg-Kristall* (*Mountain Crystal*) by Gudrun Gruen, Zurich, Switzerland. 1985. 48″ x 38″. All cotton fabrics. Hand-pieced, hand-appliquéd, hand-quilted. Inspired by the majesty of the Swiss Alps, the quiltmaker named her work *Berg-Kristall*, or *Mountain Crystal*. For the original medallion-style wall hanging, the dominant design source was a three-dimensional cube. The central medallion is a cluster of cubes symbolizing snow, or ice crystals on the mountains. The dark, jagged elements extending from the outer border into the inner ground represent the mountains, while the quilted leaves are the flora completing the environment. This completely abstract design suggests its theme by the shapes of the major design elements, rather than by its color scheme, which is composed of a striking collection of pink, orange, blue, and dark prints. Gruen began quilting in 1982, while living with relatives in Ohio. Self-taught, she joined several classes and workshops in Columbus, Ohio, to further her art. Now she is teaching others.

69. *On the Wings of November* by A. Barbara Horvath-Storms, Muntelier, Fribourg, Switzerland. 1985. 44″ x 41″. Cotton and silk fabrics. Hand-pieced, hand-quilted. An abstract, geometric study in wintry colors, this design suggests the season's harsh winds with its strong curvilinear quilting designs that recall the swooping of wings, the movement of flight. Divided between her love for both traditional quilt designs and contemporary original designs, the quiltmaker explains: "My traditional quilts are made to show the harmony and beauty of colors and printed fabrics with the best design and best possible craftsmanship in the sewing and the quilting." A professional quilter and quilting instructor whose BAHO quilt gallery deals in antique quilts and textiles, she is caught in the same dilemma that faces most artists whenever a work is sold: "One eye laughs, the other cries." The sponsor of "Swiss Quilt 85," the first international quilt exhibition in Switzerland, the quiltmaker has had one of her own quilt designs chosen for the Museum of Bern. She explains that although quilting is not a native art in Switzerland, Swiss customs may have influenced the development of Amish quilt design in America since many of the original Amish emigrated from the Canton of Bern. In that area barn doors are all painted in what is recognized today as simplified Log Cabin designs, perhaps a precursor of the graphic Center Diamond motif of many Amish quilts.

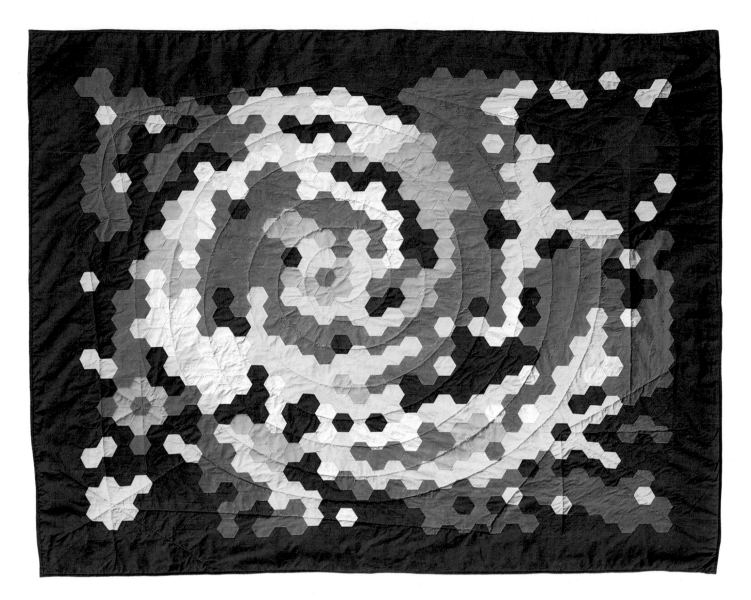

70. *La Nébuleuse* (*Nebula*) by Françoise Mermod-Fricker, Dombresson, Switzerland. 1985. 133 x 168 cm (50⅜″ x 63⅝″). Cotton fabrics. Pieced, quilted. "The hexagon in the age of interstellar travel" is the description given this quilt by its maker, whose husband helped design it while "playing around with hexagon graph paper" in his effort to represent the birth of a new star. A vivid depiction of a nebula giving birth to new stars, this quilt's vivid center colors become less brilliant as they reach the edge of the spiral galaxy and the material of the new stellar system cools down. "This quilt was rather tedious to piece, as I had to follow a coded pattern to place each color patch in the right place, and you could not see the overall end effect until the piece was complete," says the quiltmaker. She was obviously successful in her effort, because the finished quilt now hangs in her husband's office. What fascinates this quiltmaker about quilting is the play of color and shape and how they interact to create a new surface. "And I *love* to handle fabric; it is soothing," she asserts.

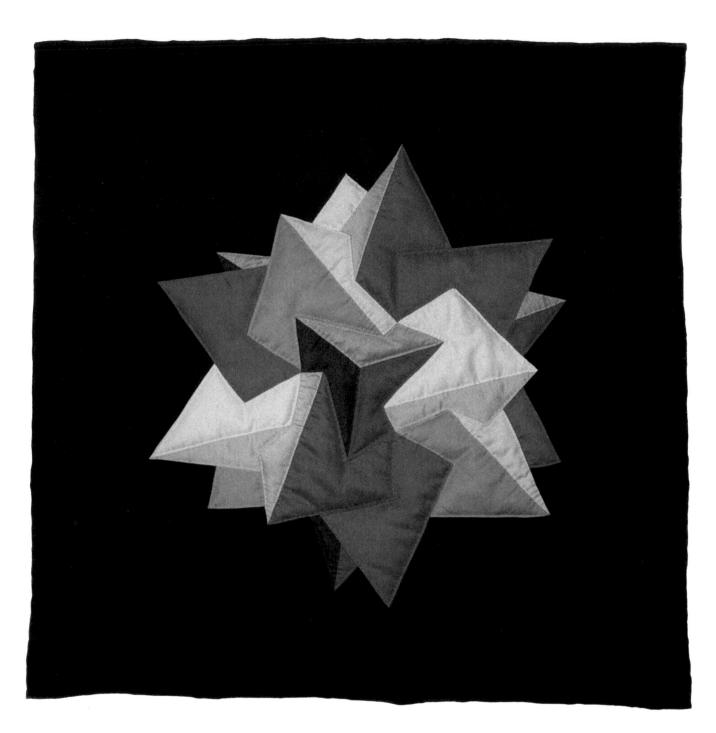

71. *Krypton* by Isabelle Schneider, Hauterive, Switzerland. 1984. 75 x 75 cm (28⅞″ x 28⅞″). All cotton fabrics, polyester filling. Machine-pieced, hand-quilted. This square, black quilt, with its multicolored center medallion in the form of a dodecahedron, is based on a mathematical drawing in *Scientific American* magazine that the quiltmaker saw years ago and couldn't forget. "I thought about it many times and always put it aside again, discouraged by all that intricate piecing," she explains. Finally, with the help of family and friends, enlarging the original drawing, casting the shadows, and selecting the colors were accomplished. Schneider pieced the intricate design by working "around the clock" for two days. Although it is not at first apparent, no two pieces of this quilt are alike. "Most of the pieces are five-sided, with just as many inset corners," she notes. "I had real nightmares of creating a many-faced parachute-looking thing which couldn't lie flat!" The quiltmaker has had her work exhibited in several shows in Switzerland and Germany.

72. *Triangles II / Three Mountains* by Sylvia Zumbach, Wetzikon, Switzerland. 1980. 93″ x 85″. Corduroy and silk fabrics. Machine-pieced and hand-quilted. The light and dark triangles of reflecting silk and matte corduroy portray sun and fog on three mountains and are arranged in wide horizontal bands. The quilt design is meant to express the light and shade, cheerfulness and sorrow that are a part of life in the mountains. "My quilts are the result of my love of classic simplicity, of my pictorial many-layered ideas, and of my joy in mastering manual techniques," says this Swiss artist and quiltmaker. "I have tried to fit my complicated picture-ideas into the strict structures of American quilts," she adds. "The management of the divisions in the large surface areas and the possibility of a technically clean-cut and simple translation from paint to textile make the patchwork patterns really wonderful," she notes. A painter who occasionally tried to transfer an idea into textiles by weaving or sewing, the designer in 1960 started to work seriously with textiles, teaching herself appliqué and piecing. In 1972, she saw an exhibition of American quilts for the first time, and between that time and the present she has completed more than thirty. She is a member of the Society of Swiss Women Artists and her work has been pictured on the cover of *Textilforum*, a German magazine.

73. *Tahitian Roses*, Marie Carr, owner, Tahiti. Quiltmaker unknown. 84″ x 84″. Hand-appliquéd. This large square piece is a beautiful example of a Tahitian quilt, a *tifaifai*. Its bright red combined with light and dark green are the colors of the lush island foliage, and the roses are constructed using a variation of the Hawaiian *cut-paper appliqué* technique. In this method, paper is folded into quarters, then cut into an intricate design. When the paper is unfolded, the design of the quilt is revealed for the first time. Quilts made by this method are usually finished with "ripple" quilting or "echo" quilting, in which the stitches follow the outline of the design elements. This bold floral design is typical of Tahitian work. Quilting was most probably introduced into the Polynesian islands by American missionaries in the mid-nineteenth century. Before the islanders had access to woven cloth, garments were made of fiber produced by a felting process, using the treated inner bark of a native mulberry tree. The resulting unwoven cloth was pounded into shape and needed no sewing. When the missionaries brought with them the idea of pieced quilts, they found that the island women had little patience with the idea of cutting up whole pieces of fabric into small shapes and then sewing them back together again to form another whole. Instead they preferred to work with large appliqué designs emphasizing either flowers or nature, and this preference has extended to today's quilters.

74. *Glorious Lady Freedom* by Moneca Calvert, Carmichael, California, U.S.A. 1985–1986. 72″ x 71½″. Cotton, cotton blends, polyester, and linen fabrics. Pieced, appliquéd, hand-quilted. A spectacular statement of the American spirit, this quilt was the Grand Prize winner in the quilt contest held to celebrate the Statue of Liberty's Centennial. Using the words of "America the Beautiful" as her inspiration, the quiltmaker has captured the purple mountains' majesty, the spacious skies, and amber waves of grain so celebrated by that stirring anthem. The brooding figure of Lady Liberty herself looms over the countryside with torch held high, and is enveloped in our rippling flag. The color selected for the statue reflects the patina that has developed over the last 100 years of her existence in New York Harbor. The quiltmaker created her design in six months, after remembering a 1982 visit to the statue which had a profound effect on her own personal self-image as an American. "If I had not seen that statue myself, I could not have done this quilt," she recalls. The design features both enormous patriotic appeal and technical innovation, certainly a winning combination in any land.

75. *Shiraz* by Judy P. Cloninger, Seabrook, Texas, U.S.A. 1983. 96″ x 69″. Cotton fabric. Hand-pieced, hand-quilted. "*Shiraz* blends designs from the Eastern Oriental rug with techniques of the traditional American quilt," explains the quiltmaker. "From a comparison of quilts and rugs, I found the two art forms had many intrinsic similarities and historically had developed the same design formats." Some of the Oriental influences incorporated into this quilt include using stepped sides on the edges of the square blocks as a transition from one color to the next; blending neutrals with the main colors to create harmony; employing border design variations; varying the symmetry; and utilizing an unusual eight-pointed star design. The subtle palette of rusts, blues, and neutral shades has been manipulated to produce designs within designs and optical illusions. The quiltmaker, who lives in the Southwest, near Houston, credits the city's abundance of quilt-related influences—including shops, the annual International Quilt Festival, and a large guild—with making it "easy to become immersed in the creative world of quiltmaking." Although her work reflects her admiration for the traditional American quilt, her primary goal is to produce aesthetically pleasing designs. "Striving to create an artistic abstract design transcends political, religious, and geographical boundaries. One craftsman can speak to another across the barriers of time, space, and philosophy." This work won the three top awards at the Houston Quilt Festival in 1983, the only time that any one quilt has been so honored.

76. *Cherokee Trail of Tears* by Chris Wolf Edmonds, Lawrence, Kansas, U.S.A. 82″ x 58″. Cotton fabrics. Machine-pieced, hand-appliquéd, hand-quilted. Long before American colonization, the Cherokee Indians controlled immense lands, but through a series of disadvantageous treaties with the U.S. government, the original holdings were reduced by about half. Ten years after the Cherokees had developed their own alphabet, making them the only Indian nation able to read and write in their native tongue, they were forcibly driven from their homes and marched westward. More than 4,000 of them died on that terrible journey of more than a year, known later as "The Trail Where They Cried." This quilt tells that story. The seated figure represents the despair of the "Trail of Tears," while the figure of the woman and child represent the will to survive and rebuild. Two teardrops are formed by the shapes of the head and hair of the woman and the blanket and body of the child. Above, the figure of Sequoyah, who developed the Cherokee alphabet, raises his quill; and hovering high is the legendary phoenix, representing the ability of the Cherokee nation to rejuvenate itself. The quiltmaker developed a national reputation for her detailed picture quilts, including *George Washington at Valley Forge* and *Freedom Rider*. She began to make quilts as "beautiful covers for my family's beds," but soon began to view her quiltmaking as her primary source of artistic expression.

77. *Stravinsky's Rite* by Alison Goss, Modesto, California, U.S.A. 1985. 60″ x 76″. Cotton fabrics. Machine-pieced, hand-quilted. Creating this quilt as a challenge to interpret a piece of music in fabric, the quiltmaker found herself fascinated with the process of design, which required a blending of both intellectual and creative expression. She chose to interpret Stravinsky's *Rite of Spring* in this design, created by constructing several sets of strips for strip-piecing, cutting them into varying widths, and pinning them to her work wall. The entire design was created on the wall before a single stitch was taken. "It was important to me to show both the beauty and the violence in the music, as well as its rhythmic complexity. I became intensely involved with the music." Extensive research into Stravinsky's work helped her to reflect these concepts more accurately in her design. "I approached the design process as he approached the process of composing music," she adds. The elegance of the colors, the way they flow through the quilt, the symbolic peaks and valleys of the design, all have direct kinship to musical composition. The quiltmaker, whose trademark is her development of strip-piecing that resembles Bargello or flame-stitch needlework, is self-taught. *Stravinsky's Rite* won Best of Show at the 1985 judged show of the American/International Quilt Association in Houston, Texas.

78. *Hilltown* by Nancy Halpern, Natick, Massachusetts, U.S.A. 1980. 73″ x 71″. Cotton and cotton-blend fabrics. Machine-pieced, hand-quilted. Houses perch on hillsides, claiming their rightful places within the rocky environment, in this exciting blend of architecture and quiltmaking. The quiltmaker, a former student of architecture who continues a lifelong love affair with the angles and planes of buildings as translated to geometric pieces destined for quilts, explains that this quilt "brought my life full circle." Fascinated with "regional vernacular architecture"—especially hilltowns—she turned to the construction of quilts as building another form of shelter "to warm body and spirit." Noted as one of the United States' most innovative contemporary quiltmakers, the New England designer comments: "*Hilltown* gives me a sense of place, pleasure in recombining the scattered elements of my life, and reassurance at the gentle fit of town to land, quilt to hand."

79. *Barefoot and Pregnant* by Jean Ray Laury, Clovis, California, U.S.A. 1985. 47″ x 47″. Silk-screen printed, hand-painted, pieced, hand-quilted. Inspired to indignation by a newspaper report of the stereotyped sentiments of a state politician, the quiltmaker turned to her art to create a rebuttal of old-fashioned thinking that keeps women in boxes not of their own making. The quilt makes a humorous, positive statement on women's rights that might be impossible except in a nation that guarantees both the right to dissent and the right to free speech. "The daily bombardment of words from newspapers, billboards, ads, mail, radio and television sometimes overloads our circuits so that we become oblivious to what is being said. Or, in self-defense, we block out what is too difficult or too painful to hear. Yet there are some statements I hope everyone will hear ... and giving them visual form helps us 'hear' them. I find the combination of images and words irresistible." The quiltmaker's witty, contemporary approach to design is a product of both the Midwest, where she grew up, and the West Coast, where she lives and works. "Perhaps the influence of the West Coast on my work has been more attitudinal or philosophical—certainly the acceptance of diversity allows me to do quilts that might seem bizarre elsewhere," she points out. Today the author of more than a dozen books on quilting and stitchery, she started quilting, or "drawing in fabric," because she was "intrigued by the graphic possibilities of fabric."

80. *Techny Chimes* by Nancy Pearson, Morton Grove, Illinois, U.S.A. 1984. 52″ x 52″. Silk and cotton fabric. Hand-appliquéd and pieced. This original design, blending childhood memories, delicacy of design, and meticulous workmanship, pays tribute to antique appliqué quilts, a favorite of this midwestern quiltmaker. The elaborate, fanciful floral design could only be achieved by someone with a mastery of appliqué because the fine, twining stems and elegant detailing of the flowers require equally fine stitches. The many shades of peach used in the quilt reminded the quiltmaker of the magnificent fields of hybrid daylilies surrounding an old mission house in Techny, Illinois, near her home. "When my children were small, we would spend many peaceful afternoons there watching the goldfish in the pond. All around were fields of beautiful daylilies that Brother Charles had created. One of my favorites was a soft peach-colored one called Techny Chimes." The designer turned to quiltmaking while she spent four months waiting in a hospital, where one of her children was undergoing treatment for bone cancer. She found a magazine in the hospital lobby with directions on how to make a quilt. "I decided to try it and found that it really helped me through a difficult time." This beautiful creation, with its soft, gentle pastel colors and lively, almost whimsical design, won Best of Show in the major international competition sponsored by the American/International Quilt Association in Houston, Texas.

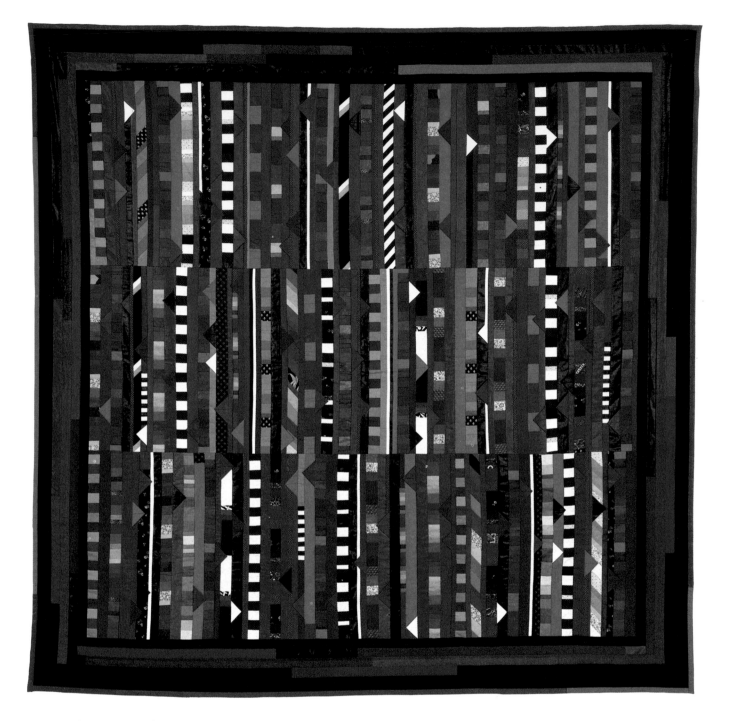

81. *Masquerade* by Yvonne Porcella, Modesto, California, U.S.A. 1982. 64" x 64". Machine-pieced. Brilliant strip-pieced colors of deep, vibrant hues spark this heavily textured design, which incorporates a traditional American design element, Prairie Points, into its surface. "I had recently purchased an antique quilt which had one-inch calico squares as the surface design element and folded triangles, Prairie Points, around the edge," explains the quiltmaker. "The small squares of lively colors were bordered with orange and black squares. I call it my Halloween quilt. *Masquerade* is based on the elements of design found in that old quilt. I used lively colors in both one-inch squares and narrow strips, as well as the triangles, and red and black fabrics." The quiltmaker, who does not work with repetitive block designs, selected one design of vertical strips of many colors and created the overall composition of nine of these blocks. "Somewhere, Nine Patch blocks are hiding, hence the name *Masquerade*," she points out. Because of the vertical set of the blocks, only the horizontal joining line is noticeable. The quiltmaker began her career as a fiber artist in the field of clothing design and has published several books on this topic featuring patchwork garments. Self-taught, she is not restricted by traditional American quilt design, but is often inspired by antique quilts.

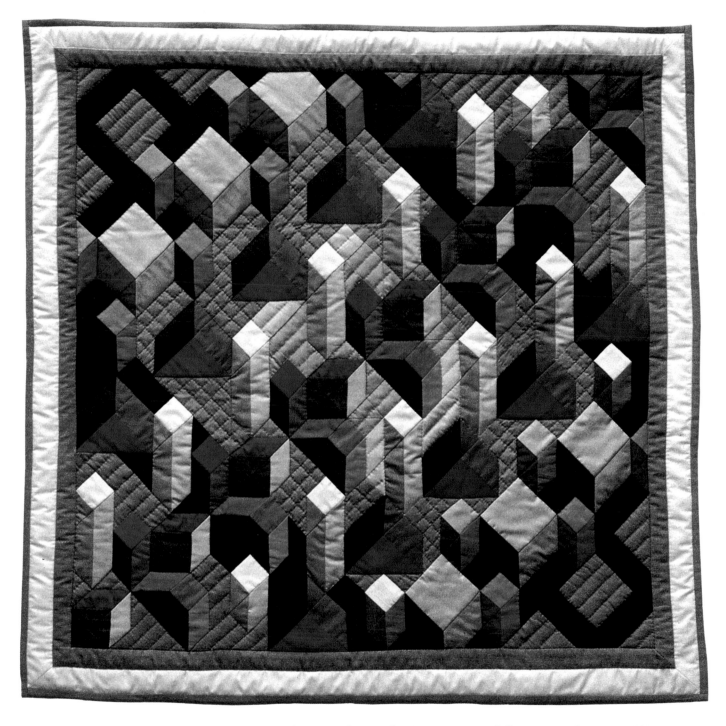

82. *Reissbrettstadt III* (*Drawing Board City III*) by Dr. Ilse Grieninger, Heidelberg, West Germany. 1985. 100 x 100 cm (37⅞″ x 37⅞′). Pieced, hand-quilted. The purity of geometric forms—the square, the triangle, and the rhombus—is emphasized in this dramatic design, a bird's-eye view of a contemporary, even futuristic city. The exclusive use of these three basic forms creates a fascinating exercise in visual restraint. "I try to achieve or dissolve tension in my work through color developments or contrasts, light-dark effects, transparency effects, and perspective," states the quiltmaker. "I include the quilting line more and more in my compositions to structure surfaces and emphasize perspective." The quilting design used in this piece is simple, yet effective in emphasizing the sharp geometric lines and the optical effect created by the selection of colors. What appears to be arbitrary placement of form and color is actually a formal progression of design in diagonal lines. "I learned about patchwork in 1980 when I attended a show in the Max Berk Textilmuseum in Heidelberg. I was so fascinated by the quilts that I immediately enrolled in a course at the museum. I later began to develop my own designs because I found the framework of traditional patterns too narrow for me."

83. *Bewegung* (*Movement*) by Inge Hueber, Cologne, West Germany. 1983. 263 x 166 cm (99⅝″ x 62⅞″). Cotton fabrics, polyester batting. Machine-pieced, hand-quilted. Employing the technique of Seminole piecing for the first time, the quiltmaker has created a visual treat, full of dimension, imagination, motion, and depth. To obtain the vast array of subtle hues required for such a design, she used scraps of hand-dyed cotton fabric that she had left over from other projects. She pieced the colored fabrics together irregularly to form long strips, then cut the strips diagonally and recombined them to form "a red stream of motion." "For me, block patchwork expresses more traditional qualities, and the women of former days found the very best possibilities of doing it," the quiltmaker states. "I try to find new patchwork ways to express my searching, my definition of life, and to me, that means movement." Self-taught, her work has been exhibited in Quilt Biennale at the Max Berk Textilmuseum in Heidelberg.

84. *Up and Down* by Inge Hueber, Cologne, West Germany. 1984. 200 x 250 cm (75¾″ x 94¹¹/₁₆″). Cotton fabrics, polyester batting. Machine-pieced, hand-quilted. "Whereas *Movement* is formed of scraps, *Up and Down* is planned more strictly," explains the quiltmaker. "I chose only three colors (red, blue, beige) in different shades, from dark to light. Then I cut them in strips and long triangles to get the curves, the 'up and down.'" The quilt reflects meticulous workmanship in its exact piecing, and the flowing lines of the quilting design enhance the curved effect.

85. *Windsurfing 83* by Irene Kahmann, Groebenzell, West Germany. 1984. 125 x 180 cm (47⅜″ x 68³/₁₆″). Cotton and silk fabrics. Machine-pieced, hand-quilted. Colorful sails dot the sunlit water in this abstract pictorial quilt, created after the quiltmaker and her family had spent a week's vacation at Lake Garda, Italy, where windsurfing is especially popular because of the favorable winds for sailing. This sport has become very popular with German families, according to the quiltmaker, whose husband and two sons are active participants. In this quilt, slanting rays of sunlight beckon the eye to the focal point of the largest sail, while the selection of deeper hues of blue accurately depicts the portions of the lake that still lie in the shade. The quilting design is particularly well-conceived: curving breezes sweep down from the surrounding mountains to catch the sails and send them flying, and gentle waves and currents are quilted into the lake depths. It is interesting to note that the majority of this quilt has been pieced from one basic pattern piece—a rectangle approximately 1″ wide, cut in different lengths, similar to a basic Log Cabin piece. The quiltmaker became interested in quilts during her family's stay in Raleigh, North Carolina, in 1975–1977 and enrolled in classes. When she returned to Germany, she started teaching quilting, and now sees quilting firmly established in that country. The quiltmaker is the author of a German quilting book, *Patchwork and Quilters.*

86. *Bryce Canyon* by Irene Kahmann, Groebenzell, West Germany. 1983. 72″ x 66″. Cotton fabrics. Hand-pieced, hand-quilted. The dramatic image of Utah's Bryce Canyon stayed in this quiltmaker's mind for several years after her visit to the United States, long enough for her to collect the large assortment of prints and solids required to produce this quilt. There are more than 900 pieces in her work, part of which is based on a triangular version of the traditional Log Cabin design. "I was so impressed to see the power of the persistence of forces that had shaped the earth's surface in plateaus and sculptured rocks," she comments. "All of this spreads out from the rim as far as the eye can see, until far in the distance, it blends into the expansive landscape of plateaus, dark with evergreen forests."

87. *Grapefruit* by Friederike Kohlhaussen, Bad Homburg, West Germany. 1984. 156 x 184 cm (59^1/$_{16}$″ x 69^{11}/$_{16}$″).
All cotton fabrics. Machine-pieced and hand-quilted. This lush, heavily quilted quilt in crisp, citrus shades of
yellows, oranges, and greens utilizes curved-seam piecing to produce the abstract image. Its maker learned
quilting between 1979–1981 when she was living in Greenwich, Connecticut, and took classes at the YWCA. She
is a former student of Maria Belden, who has taught quilting to many women from other countries. The artist has
taught patchwork and quilting in Bad Homburg for the past four years and is a member of an active quilting
group.

88. *Die Flüsse Meiner Heimat* (*The Rivers of My Homeland*) by Liesel Niesner, Osnabrück, West Germany. 1985. 124 x 165 cm (46¹⁵/₁₆″ x 62½″). All cotton fabrics. Machine-pieced, hand-quilted. The undulating, flowing curves of this design, selected to recall the clear German rivers of the quiltmaker's youth, create the effect of the river's current. The light, bright colors used in the center represent the shallows of the river, where the sunlight plays on the water, while the dark, rich colors depict the still depths of the water in the shade of the riverbank. "Now the colours of the rivers of my homeland are not so clear as earlier," the quiltmaker states with regret. "As a child, I could swim in any river or brook without hesitation, and I deeply regret that this grew impossible for my children. So this quilt is the first in a remembrance of earlier days." Just a few years ago, recalls this designer, almost no one in West Germany had ever heard the word *patchwork*. If people ask her today for a German word to describe what a patchwork quilt is, she can only reply that no such word exists in the German language. Recently, however, quilting has grown much more popular in Germany, with books and exhibitions featuring it. Fascinated when her fifteen-year-old daughter tried patchwork just for fun in 1978, the quilter began with a patchwork pillow, and "from that time I was imprisoned by patchwork," she recalls. She is a member of the Bundesverband Kunsthandwerk Deutschland and has had her work exhibited in the 1984 Quilt Biennale in Heidelberg. In the last seven years, she has made about fifty-five quilts.

89. *Auf Meinen Krummen Streifen* (*On My Crooked Stripes*) by Erika Odemer, Munich, West Germany. 260 x 180 cm (98½" x 68³/₁₆"). Cotton fabrics. Pieced, hand-quilted. Ignoring the boundaries of its borders, this piece refuses to be confined in a formal structure. It creates the impression of multihued braids when viewed at a distance. The piece is hand-quilted in a spiral pattern that also crosses the boundaries of the pieced design to swirl at will. Working with a sumptuous palette of pinks, fuchsias, mauves, and blues in cotton chintz, the quilt-maker has produced a striking contemporary piece that indicates the new directions quiltmaking is going in West Germany. This quiltmaker, according to one of her colleagues, is a new face on the European quiltmaking scene.

90. *Variation #1* by Katherine Picot, Baden-Baden, West Germany. 1983. 160 x 160 cm (60½″ x 60½″). Cotton and satin fabrics. Hand-pieced, hand-quilted. Strong shaded contrasts, the interesting construction of a circular form from basic triangles and squares, and abstract imagery characterize this stunning quilt, the designer's first departure from tradition. It was inspired by an effect obtained in a traditional quilt, however, one which she "stared at every morning upon awakening and which gave me the idea for the circular development of the colors." *Variation #1* is based on the combination of traditionally pieced blocks set into an allover design in which only the colors change, moving from the deep red center out to pale pinks and white, and then moving into plum shades that darken to a deep black-blue. Both satin and polished cotton are used to emphasize the play of light on the surface of the quilt. Although the quiltmaker is an American, heir to the rich quilting heritage of her ancestors, she did not learn patchwork and quilting until she was living in Europe. During her first pregnancy, a patchwork skirt designed by Yves St. Laurent served as her inspiration to learn this needle art. She taught herself the techniques she employs so masterfully, and has gone on to teach many German women to quilt. She was responsible for contacting many of the German textile artists whose work is pictured in this book.

91. *Sunburst* by Christl Tumat, Munich, West Germany. 1980. 63″ x 63″. Cotton fabrics. Machine-pieced and hand-quilted. A brilliant explosion of yellows and golds, with a hot core of reds shading to darker colors, is contained by the black edges of this quilt. A contemporary piece, this work gives its maker a chance to showcase her quiltmaking skills as well as her avant-garde design sensibility. The quiltmaker first became acquainted with American quilts when she visited an Amish family in Ohio during a trip to the United States. "This wonderful handwork fascinated me," she comments, "and I thought I should try something similar. When I started working in 1975, I was the only person doing quilting in Munich." However, she was not a novice to patchwork, having learned hexagonal English piecing as a child from a grand-aunt who had herself learned from an English governess.

92. *Herbst (Autumn)* by Doris Winter, Heidelberg, West Germany. 96 x 140 cm (36⅜″ x 53″). Silk fabrics. The rich surface of this piece is created from one-of-a-kind silk fabrics that this innovative quiltmaker had hand-dyed to her specifications by a German artist, a collaboration that she employs frequently in her work because it allows her to focus on experimentation with her quilting techniques. Warm reds and cool darks are juxtaposed in this piece, creating an interesting surface tension. Although her design is based on the traditional Tumbling Blocks pattern, her innovative use of color has completely altered the visual effect of this design. The quilting creates a third dimension to the quilt. The quiltmaker has been very active in developing interest in quilting in West Germany. Daughter of the man who purchased an old church outside of Heidelberg and transformed it into the Max Berk Textilmuseum, she has organized the first and second Quilt Biennales at the museum. She learned quilting in Germany from Katherine Picot, whose work is shown in figure 90.

APPENDIX

COMMENTS BY
MARY PENDERS AND BARBARA HORVATH
ON CONTEMPORARY QUILTING

AUSTRALIA

To experience Australia's unique landscape of intense color and light is to understand the strong influence of the natural world upon that continent's art. While Australian quilters followed the English method of patchwork well into the 1970s, the American Bicentennial was influential in popularizing American techniques and designs. Following this revival, with its phenomenal growth of quilting throughout this vast country, Australian quilt artists have been inspired to produce quilts that reflect uniquely Australian themes, designs, and experiences.

Combining love of color with love of nature, many quilts portray the underlying complexity of the bush landscape, the intense coloration of the tropics, or the effect of the light patterns of western Australia. Many quiltmakers demonstrate a strong Japanese influence in both fabric and composition; others display the influence of the Aboriginal culture with stylized designs and rich earth colors. In seeking to develop their own heritage, women who are frequently working in isolation are bold in their experimentation with a wide variety of textiles, which gives their quilts unusual textures and innovative fabric combinations. While these women are intensely interested in American quilts and quiltmakers, they are most responsive to techniques that can lead them toward the vision of a recognized Australian style.

HOLLAND

Holland is not only windmills and wooden shoes but also warm, hospitable people who, reflecting the Dutch character, are accepting and tolerant of all forms of quiltmaking. Just as the seventeenth-century architecture of Amsterdam exists harmoniously alongside striking contemporary design, so also are Dutch quilters comfortable with both the American heritage and the simultaneous development of a characteristic Dutch style of quilting.

Quilters are beginning to use Dutch fabrics, which

may incorporate cottons from traditional clothing worn for generations. For example, fabrics used in the women's dresses in the fishing village of Spakenburg are made of intense, vibrant hues of purple and red that are combined with black in stunning prints. It is fascinating to observe these women going about their daily errands on their bicycles, adorned in the rich regional dress that displays these unusual textiles. Increasingly, these fabrics are finding their way into the traditional patterns favored by Dutch quilters; soon they will inspire designs that display the virtuosity of a country that has produced the diverse art of Rembrandt, Van Gogh, and Mondrian.

NEW ZEALAND

Across the varied and stunning landscapes of New Zealand, many lives are committed to fabric art. New Zealand abounds with craftspersons producing a vast array of high-quality work in a variety of media. Quilters are influenced by the physical beauty and climate of a maritime nation where no one lives far from the sight and sound of the sea. Often their work reflects the inspiration of the Maori design heritage. As in Australia, many quilters work in relative isolation, with no access to quilting shops and traditional supplies. In these instances, from necessity there has evolved work of remarkable originality, in both design and use of fabric. New Zealand quilts tend to express a strong individual identity.

Also notable about quiltmaking in New Zealand is the large number of quilters listed in the national crafts directory who make quilts for sale and on commission. In New Zealand, quilts and weaving and pottery seem to be honored and cherished by the general population, and quiltmaking, for many individuals, is progressing from a passionate avocation to a dedicated occupation.

SWITZERLAND

In Switzerland, the traditional quilt holds a strong attraction because of the orderliness of its beauty. It is emulated by many, because without the great examples of traditional quilts, there would be no continuation. Yet the Swiss quilters imbue each piece with their own contemporary sense of color and design, experimenting with great pleasure, while still remembering those important tiny stitches, the careful elaboration, and the placement of the right color in the right place. They strive not for speed, even in this day of widespread interest in quick methods, but instead they are more interested in creating an impression of depth.

TAHITI

When Paul Gauguin fled to Tahiti in 1891, he adopted the unchanging existence of the Maoris. Almost one hundred years later, this island paradise is beset by such late twentieth-century ills as pollution and traffic jams. In the midst of tourist-scarred Papeete can be found the thatch-roofed building of the Tahitian artisans with its long clothesline hung with quilts. And what splendid quilts!

Gauguin wrote: "The natural scents intoxicate me and inspire me with dreams of violent harmonies." Here were the yellows of his leaves, the reds of his streams, the purples of his meadows—violent harmonies in large appliqué shapes, which give a marvelous purity to the dense colors. The harmonious lines reflect the natural rhythms of the flora of the island. There is no need in the warmth of the tropics for filler in the quilts, so they are backed but not always quilted. This is a suitable adaptation for the Tahitian home, whose walls are open from window level to the roof. Within these dwellings, one may glimpse the "violent harmonies" in their decoration. The women who make quilts in their homes display the faces Paul Gauguin painted; they are beautiful, dignified, and gracious in their acceptance of the praises of a stranger who fell in love with their quilts.

WEST GERMANY

The quilts of West Germany are a revelation in the unusual independence of their designs. Throughout the Federal Republic, women are designing geometric quilts that are not derivative and that often appear strikingly original. There is an intellectual vitality in German quilts. Whereas colors tend to be subdued, designs are graphic and bold. Textures are greatly varied. In many instances, quilt artists appear to have been influenced by the German Expressionist painters, who represented their ideas and emotions symbolically in order to express experiences beneath the surface. This concept has freed the quiltmaker to render the intangible, the imagined, and the nonrealistic within the dimensions of fabric art. There is a tension in many of the German quilts that immediately draws the viewer toward the personality and the imagination of the quilter, as if she were seeking to share her particular vision.

PHOTOGRAPH AND PUBLICATION CREDITS

Autumn Winds by Margaret E. Hannaford (fig. 1). Published in *Quilting Australia*.

Australian Birds by Margaret Rolfe (fig. 4). Published in *Australian Patchwork Designs*.

Barrier Reef by Jane Wilson (fig. 7). Photograph by Jerry DeFelice.

Little Town in Minas Gerais by Barbara Schaeffter (fig. 10). Photograph by Jerry DeFelice.

Don's Quilt by Winifrede Burry (fig. 13). Photograph by Donald Standfield. Published in *Canada Quilts Magazine*.

Communication by Winifrede Burry (fig. 14). Photograph by Donald Standfield. Published in *Canada Quilts Magazine*.

The Peace Quilt by Valerie Hearder (fig. 15). Photograph by Valerie Hearder.

Reflections and Illusions III by Marilyn Stothers (fig. 18). Photograph by Ernest Mayer.

Reflections and Illusions IV by Marilyn Stothers (fig. 19). Photograph by Ernest Mayer.

Curving Cubes II by Marilyn Stothers (fig. 20). Photograph by Ernest Mayer.

Bruderkransen by Anne Marie Harrison and the Patchwork Fonden (fig. 22). Published in Patchwork Foundation Exhibition Catalog 1984.

Victoria and Albert by Lotte Jacobsen (fig. 23). Published in *Patchwork & Appliqué*.

Colourwash Framed I by Deirdre Amsden (fig. 25). Photograph by Jerry DeFelice. Published in *Textilforum 1984*.

Colourwash Framed II by Deirdre Amsden (fig. 26). Published in *Quiltmaking in Patchwork & Appliqué*.

Memories of Suffolk by Jacqueline R. Claiborne (fig. 28). Published in *Virginia Pilot* newspaper (Norfolk, Virginia).

Royal Wedding by Gillian Clarke (fig. 29). Published in *Patchwork Mania*.

Oxfam by Gillian Clarke (fig. 30). Published in *Patchwork Mania*.

Rainbow Lattice by Sheila Wells (fig. 33). Photograph by Valerie Campbell. Published in *Strip Patchwork*.

The Paris Presentation Quilt by Le Patchwork Club de France (fig. 35). Photograph by Le Livre Studio. Published in *Patchworks*.

Memory Without End by Kitty van Rhijn-Boersema (fig. 37). Photograph by Mary Penders.

Catharina's Compass by Rina Schouten-Vergunst (fig. 38). Photograph by Mary Penders.

Hope by Geeta Khandelwal (fig. 39). Photograph by Jerry DeFelice.

Anniversary Quilt by Margaret McClintock Slutz (fig. 40). Photograph by Jerry DeFelice.

Flaming Drum by Sanae Hattori (fig. 43). Published in *The Quilt Japan*.

Soaring Crane by Sanae Hattori (fig. 44). Published in *The Quilt Japan* and in *Fujin Gaho*.

Weeping Cherry Branches by Sanae Hattori (fig. 45). Published in *The Quilt Japan* and in *Patchwork Quilt Tsūshin*.

Crane by Hiroko Kawahito (fig. 47). Published in *Patchwork Quilt Tsūshin*.

Japanese Talisman by Jill Liddell (fig. 48). Published in *Patchwork Quilt Tsūshin*.

Spring Celebration by Emi Masaoka (fig. 49). Published in *Patchwork Quilt Tsūshin*.

Kagome by Ruri Miyamoto (fig. 50). Published in *Patchwork Quilt Tsūshin*.

Peony by Takako Morohashi (fig. 51). Published in *Patchwork Quilt Tsūshin*.

Kyoto by Hiroko Nakamura (fig. 52). Published in *Patchwork Quilt Tsūshin*.

Antique Sashiko Jacket owned by Takae Onoyama (fig. 53). Published in *Sashiko*.

Kamon Sampler by Yukiko Saito (fig. 54). Published in *Patchwork Quilt Tsūshin*.

Game of Shells by Masako Satoh (fig. 55). Published in *Patchwork Quilt Tsūshin*.

Sakura Fuji by Keiko Yoshida (fig. 56). Published in *Patchwork Quilt Tsūshin*.

Pukerua Bay Beach by Marge Hurst (fig. 59). Photograph by Jerry DeFelice.

Evocation by The Wednesday Night Group (fig. 60). Published in *Threads (New Zealand)*.

Oil Production in Deep Waters by Anne-Donia Bruun Hafskjold (fig. 61). Photograph by Roar Lange.

Grand Canyon by Christine Berry (fig. 62). Published in *Quilter's Newsletter Magazine*.

On the Wings of November by A. Barbara Horvath-Storms (fig. 69). Photograph by Walter German.

Glorious Lady Freedom by Moneca Calvert (fig. 74). Photograph by Schecter Lee. Published in *All Flags Flying*.

Shiraz by Judy P. Cloninger (fig. 75). Photograph by John Hunt.

Cherokee Trail of Tears by Chris Wolf Edmonds (fig. 76). Photograph by Robert Hale.

Stravinsky's Rite by Alison Goss (fig. 77). Photograph by Sharon Risedorph. Published in *American Quilter Magazine* (Spring 1986 and Fall 1986) and in American Quilter Society's *Quilt Art 1987 Engagement Calendar*.

Hilltown by Nancy Halpern (fig. 78). Photograph by Jon Blumb. Published in *Quilter's Newsletter Magazine*.

Techny Chimes by Nancy Pearson (fig. 80). Photograph by Jerry DeFelice.

Masquerade by Yvonne Porcella (fig. 81). Photograph by Jon Blumb.

Sunburst by Christl Tumat (fig. 91). Published in *Patchwork und Appli-kationen*.

Dep. Leg. B-29,708-86